# PORN & PONG

## How Grand Theft Auto, Tomb Raider and Other Sexy Games Changed Our Culture

Feral House

Feral House
1240 W. Sims Way Ste. 124
Port Townsend, WA  98368
Send S.A.S.E. for free catalogue of publications

info@feralhouse.com
www.feralhouse.com

10 9 8 7 6 5 4 3 2 1

"Pornography is the secret engine that drives the adoption of most modern technology, videogames included. By connecting the dots (or rather, pixels) between interactive media and that most interactive of human experiences, Brown shows the pivotal role erotic content has played in the evolution of this new medium, as well as the furor and controversy it inevitably stirs up."

—Scott Alexander, Senior Editor, *Playboy*

"A stimulating look at two of today's most controversial subjects... Sure to amaze and titillate anyone who's ever hoisted a videogame controller."

—Scott Steinberg, CNN Tech Correspondent
and author of *Videogame Marketing and PR*

"Damon Brown tells the tale of the marriage of pop culture, video games, and porn with a geek's glee and a historian's attention to detail."

—Audacia Ray, Author of *Naked on the Internet:
Hookups, Downloads and Cashing In on Internet Sexploration*

"I have no idea why Damon Brown included Leisure Suit Larry in this book about all those dirty games, but I must agree with the U.S. Supreme Court: I can't define a good game, but I know one when I see one!"

—Al Lowe, Creator of *Leisure Suit Larry*, www.allowe.com

"A thorough, meticulously researched history of video games and other adult entertainment, providing much food for thought about a generation that grew up taking all of it for granted. Just how many of today's best games do we owe to sex, anyway?"

—Regina Lynn, Wired.com Sex Drive columnist
and author of *The Sexual Revolution 2.0*

**TO MOM, MY SUPPORT**
**TO JANE, MY GUIDE**
**&**
**TO PARUL, MY LOVE**

# CONTENTS

# FOREPLAY

## A FOREWORD
## BY JON M. GIBSON

Growing up, I was sexually retarded.

The videogame industry now is about as stupid I was then about sex.

And I was really fucking stupid.

When I was eight, I was caught playing doctor with a girl across the street. We were merely "examining" each other's parts, but her younger sister still ratted us out. That same year, I began forcefully sleeping on top of my hardons, convinced that half-mast was the status quo and that my dick pointing dead north was somehow freakish. As a ten year old, I waited until my dad blacked out with an empty bottle of Jack in his hand, then hijacked the remote to watch awkwardly scripted pay-per-view porn like *Dinosaur Island* on the illegal "black box" in the living room. I always felt like God was judging me when I jerked off — it's like he was mounted on my conscience, tisk tisking me from above. In seventh grade, our sex ed teacher suggested "not wearing sweatpants anymore, because they make erections harder to conceal. Jeans are much better." I thought blowjobs meant someone actually blew into your peehole. My first kiss at 15 was an accident — the result of my friend Dobie saying, "Why don't you two just make out already?" So we did… awkwardly. I lost my virginity in a hot tub at 17. We broke into our apartment complex's Recreation Building, started hooking up, got naked, and thought it would be sexy, like in an R-rated movie.

It wasn't.

Since puberty, I had collected all these fragments of sexual knowledge. I could have filled a dozen bookbags, but still, none of it made any sort of sense. It was like a puzzle that's all sky, but no clouds.

Howard Hughes solved that one way back in 1928 filming *Hell's Angels*. After wasting a full year and spending millions to shoot forty-five biplanes against a weather-less sky at Mines Field in Inglewood (now LAX) and Caddo Field in Van Nuys, Hughes realized that without clouds, you couldn't really tell how fast the planes were flying. The dogfights appeared almost static. They were pathetic. So in October 1928, he bankrolled a move to Oakland airfield near San Francisco in search of those much-important cotton balls in the sky.

See, it's these little details that are indispensable — the shit you never think about. *Hell's Angels* grossed $8 million at the box office (the equivalent of a movie now grossing about $100 mil). It was a hit, no thanks to performances by stars like Jean Harlow, but because the aerial stunts were so damn awesome.

The clouds were what made that badass ballet of dozens of bi-planes swooping, diving, and dodging each other possible.

Hughes was an innovator — the slickest of problem-solvers — while most filmmakers of the era were like I was during puberty: blind. The little stuff (like clouds) is invisible to the audience when they're focusing on the cool shit (like planes)... but the clouds are still essential. Other directors would have settled for no clouds, just to save a buck.

This is incredibly naïve.

It's like thinking that sex is all about boobs and ass — the confused, childish notions of a teenager's Sexpedia. (Hell, I used to firmly believe that the vagina was located two inches above where it actually is.)

This is precisely how the videogame industry regards sex.

Like a stupid fucking teenager.

Lara Croft and her watermelon tits, *BMX XXX* and its barebacked riders, and *God of War* with its thrusting mini-game — all sky, no clouds.

The correct order is clouds, then sky. Then planes.

Until the game industry realizes this, it'll forever be trapped in puberty. Which, looking back now with the knowledge I've gained since my sexual awakening... well, it's incredibly embarrassing.

Humiliating, even.

But videogames are young (born: 1958) compared to literature, film, fine art, music, and all sorts of other age-old media — a proverbial drop in the gigantic ocean of culture; amoebas, barely evolved. Gutenberg invented the printing press in 1439; and the guitar came about some 5,000 years before that. Hell, pictures painted with blood on cave walls used to be the finest form of storytelling. And ever since that first smudge was made with a thumb, one of the most commonly explored topics through these means has been sexuality.

Clouds are the reason why burlesque is so impossibly hot, and why strippers strip rather than just walk onto stage totally naked. Clouds are the warm-up, the lead-in, the anticipation that propels the end product into a completely different stratosphere.

It's the kissing of the neck, the tonguing of the nipple, the rubbing of the clit with one finger then the insertion of two. It's all that sensuous touching, the turning on of the whole body. It's the under-the-table thigh massages while the waiter takes your order. It's the sly sexual banter over AIM while you're plotting the date. It's the inaugural phone call with only subtle, but all-too-telling innuendo. It's that very first glance when one of your several attempts to make eye contact is finally received.

It's the foreplay that videogames lack.

They just skip straight to the fucking, on an express to orgasm. Evidenced by horny-boy fluff like *Dead or Alive Xtreme Beach Volleyball, Playboy: The Mansion* and *The Guy Game*, boobs and booty — the McDonald's drive-thru version of sexy — are the only things that seem to matter.

The anticipation — the visual, verbal, and physical foreplay — is just as hot as the sex. Much like we get engrossed in the chase of Romeo & Juliet and the courting in Jane Austen romances, the journey is just as important as the climax. Hitchcock perfected this approach with his masterpieces of suspense; *Basic Instinct* applied those same principles to the sexual thriller. We tuned into *Friends* every week for countless seasons before Ross and Rachel ever got together, and squealed when *M*A*S*H*'s Hawkeye and Hotlips Houlihan eventually hooked up. *From Here to Eternity*, Mulder and Scully, "Stairway to Heaven," *When Harry Met Sally*, even "Bohemian Rhapsody" — all were legendary slow builds.

Sure, it's all too easy to remember *just* the orgasm — it's tremendous. However, it's adolescent to forget *how* you got there, and especially foolish to not take your time getting there.

Besides, it's natural to only focus on the planes, forgetting about the clouds entirely. Because, well, orgasms always feel spectacular. I couldn't help but ogle Lara Croft's tits, search the internet for cheat codes to unlock all the nudity in *BMX XXX*, or continuously bounce up and down for minutes on end, just to watch Kasumi's boobies jiggle in *Xtreme Beach Volleyball*.

It's enjoyable for a second… but it's worthless in the end.

My sexual awakening began when I realized that I wasn't thinking about the clouds. Maybe someone clues you in, maybe it just clicks. I just didn't consider their importance, not in the slightest. I was moron not to, because each cloud is a building block, an essential stepping-stone on the path to complete ecstasy.

Clouds are necessary, and should not be neglected.

They provide context, and without context it's just a come shot.

*Grand Theft Auto: San Andreas* addresses this on a very basic, but admirable, level. Your character in the game, Carl "CJ" Johnson, must take his lady friend, Denise, on several dates before consummating their relationship. He must endure many cut scenes and several nights of consecutive outings before Denise finally gives it up. The culmination is the infamous "Hot Coffee" mini-game that allows you to do the deed with her.

Quite simply, since it takes a while to get to the sex — especially if you're working extra-diligently for it — it's that much more satisfying.

The industry needs to recognize, and then harness, the power of clouds (a.k.a. foreplay) before we'll see a major shift in the way sexuality is portrayed in games.

That's how I became "good" at sex.

I realized the might of clouds.

And I expect to only get better, and maybe — eventually — I will proudly wear badges like "great," "spectacular" or "mind-blowing." Still, it's entirely subjective. At twenty five, I have absolutely no license to spout such things, even if my partners would gladly gift me a gold star. Knowledge is progress — knowledge is innovation — but only if you pay attention.

I know it can only get better.

Right now, though, the only adjective that comes to mind to describe how the video game industry performs at sex… well… is something no one ever wants to hear from their lover:

Awful.

Just plain awful.

Jon M. Gibson
March 2008
Los Angeles, CA

# HISTORICAL SHORTHAND

Porn and video games: It's an awkward subject for an entire book. I admit it. When confronted with why I devoted so much time and effort to it, I would retreat into the posture of academic objectivity and reply that there is a pattern, a parallel, between video games and major shifts in pop culture. After all, if we examined games as closely as their immense cultural impact merited, and not dismissed them offhand, there's no question that we'd learn far more about ourselves than yet another field trip to the symphony or the local art museum.

The big idea here is that there is nothing new under the sun. Extremist like Fox mouthpiece Bill O'Reilly talk about Internet pornography corrupting our society, the destructive power of sexy reality television and, of course, the connection between youth sexual violence and a game of *Grand Theft Auto*. While kids should be protected, it is also important to recognize that erotic expression within pop culture is hardly new. Concerns were thrown on comic books in the fifties, when artists were forced to cover their curvy vixens up and not discuss adult situations. Brutally sexual – or sexually brutal – grindhouse movies and bikini films from the likes of Russ Meyer and Roger Corman fed a generation's appetite for tempting villainesses and pseudo-sadomasochistic antics, as did film noir, blaxploitation and other film genres before and after. Today we're watching Lara Croft's breast heave in her too-tight tank top or a *Grand Theft Auto* prostitute giving our hero his money's worth. We still want dark sexual thrills through our entertainment. The only thing that has changed is the medium. If the corruption of modern society were only about sexual content, wouldn't previous generations, with their filthy comic books, exploitation films and burlesque shows, be just as dysfunctional as we are? I suspect that's the case.

This is a young subject. The modern pornography industry began just thirty five years ago, near when I was born. Modern video games also started around the same time, and the lasting impact of this cultural convergence has yet to be analyzed. This book is live coverage of two moving targets. The concepts of modern pornography and video games are evolving literally every day. Modern history is not static. *Porn & Pong* is a Polaroid, not a final assessment.

And while we won't completely understand the impact of, say, Lara Croft on our pop culture landscape until much later, the earliness and immaturity of video game eroticism makes it even more important to document this right now. When my young Gen X generation was growing up, pornography meant bootleg VCR tapes and softcore Cinemax. To the previous generation, pornography meant *Playboy* magazine and, depending on their knowledge and location, Times Square peep show booths. To their parents, it was *Faster Pussycat Kill Kill!* and, if they were lucky, elicit 35-mm films watched on expensive home projectors. Video games have had an even more explosive evolution. My grandparents weren't even exposed to modern pornography or to video games until they were in their forties. The fact that we went from *Deep Throat* and *Pong* to online prostitution and in-game virtual sex partners in three decades shows how technology is pushing us into new sexual mores as, as a result, more sexual quandaries than ever before. Does the technology of sharing intimate words on a keyboard afford us a new type of sexual connection as much as, say, phone sex lines did previously? Is a virtual working girl, pleasuring men in an online fantasy game, as criminally guilty of prostitution as the high-heeled woman walking the downtown streets? Mature video games bring these philosophical, ethical questions to the forefront, and while we're dealing with the same shit – sexual dynamics – the rapid growth of technology is creating a new world worth exploring, if not actively building ourselves.

It is also important to notice the exponential rise of actual sex in video games, and this is because of both the gaming audience and society in general. According to the Electronic Software Association, the average gamer is a thirty-five year old male, and, looking backwards, the average age has increased by one year ever year in recent memory (thirty three in 2005, thirty four in 2006, and so on). The eighties teenagers raised on Mario are now sexually-active men around the peak of the average pornography consumer – so, yeah, there is more sex in video games than ever before. Society as a whole is also on the fast track to understanding and adjusting to new sexual opportunities. Going back to the release of *Deep Throat*, the sexual world of 1972 had no herpes, VCRs, mainstream theater pornography, 1-900 numbers, softcore cable, AIDS, Internet pornography, online dating, and virtual sex (or, as it is now called, "cybering"). Wow, how much we've had to adapt! Therefore, this book is bottom heavy: eras fall between 1972 and 1995, 1996 and 2001, and 2001 and 2008, and each era has twice as many games as the previous one. It's harder than ever to follow what is new in our sex-tech crazy world. Video games are one of the few tangible mediums we can grab onto to understand who we are, where we've been and where we might be going.

My aim is to connect disregarded and ignored video games to movies, music, sex, technology and other pop culture barometers, so I picked a selection of games that were most reflective of the times. (Not every sex-oriented game is in this book. Veteran game designer Brenda Brathwaite's *Sex In Video Games*, released in 2006, gives a more thorough overview of the titles released.) I focus on titles considered games in the colloquial sense. *Grand Theft Auto* and *Tomb Raider* are discussed, but *Virtual Jenna*, a sex simulator based on porn star Jenna Jameson, is not. The exceptions I recognize are Linden Lab's *Second Life* and a handful of other virtual worlds that have made an impact on video game design as well as modern views of sex and technology. I would have loved to have mentioned every single title I came across, as there are literally hundreds, but to capture my broad idea, I had to focus my broad idea. Great software titles have been mercilessly edited out my inquiry.

I've done my best to keep a straight face while discussing digital poo, jiggling virtual bosoms and other hapless attempts at being sexy. Why? I've found that, underneath these immature gestures, we can see how well our society is evolving sexual dynamics in the new millennium. And let's be real: To better understand this period of time, future generations will not be digging out the latest Oprah book club selection, nor will they care about the art sold yesterday at Christie's or the Yo Yo Ma piece performed at the Met. Instead, they will recover old Internet pages, rusty non-biodegradable cell phones, bad Reality TV DVDs, and interactive digital entertainment. Video games will be part of our historical shorthand. We may as well start looking at them now.

— Damon Brown, July 2008, San Francisco

From the start, "pornography" named a battlefield, a place where no assertion could be made without at once summoning up its denial, where no one could distinguish value from danger because they were the same.

—WALTER KENDRICK
*The Secret Museum: Pornography in Modern Culture*

# THE PORN ERA

## (1972 – 1995)

The adage is that if you want to know where technology is going, follow the porn. Note that the saying doesn't say porn sets the pace *gracefully*. The early pornographic games are just bad movies grafted onto, at the time, an ugly looking medium with block characters and audio bleeps. The interesting part isn't that these games were made – pornographers are nothing if not capitalists—but that people actually bought these sophomoric diversions. Eighty thousand people paid fifty bucks for the first Atari 2600 porno game. Think about that for a second.

People initially supported pornographic games not for their hollowed gameplay, nor to get off on a Crayola-level representation of a woman, but because the purchase and ownership itself was a deviant act. The pure absurdity of having porn on what was then considered a kid's medium could make even the worst game attractive to the consumer. Video games themselves remained a novelty well into the nineties. Throw sex in there and you're getting some attention.

From 1972, with the launch of *Deep Throat* and *Pong*, to 1995, right before the first digital sex symbol was created, we see pornography setting the pace on how sexuality should be expressed and interpreted in video games. There is no Lara Croft, there is no *Grand Theft Auto*, and there is no great video game canon to lean on – only a joystick, *Pac-Man* and years and years of bad pornographic movies. No wonder so many of the early games were atrocious.

# SPACESHIPS

It is Summer 1972, and Linda Lovelace is giving fantastic blowjobs all across America. By relaxing her throat muscles, Lovelace puts the length of her lover's penis in her mouth and beyond, taking it all the way down to her esophagus without choking. The movie *Deep Throat* caught her sword-swallowing act on film, inspiring jokes on Johnny Carson's *The Tonight Show* and helping drive pornography to the profitable stratosphere. Filmed for forty thousand dollars, *Deep Throat* went on to make hundreds of millions in box office receipts, home videos, sexual aids and other merchandise.

*Deep Throat* played more than seventy theaters coast-to-coast, a wide release for porn. Its distributor hired couriers who would put the 35-mm film reels in the trunk of their cars, drive to the porn theaters and hand deliver the movie. The couriers would pick the reels up when the theaters finished showcasing the film (more hastily if they received a tip that a FBI raid was planned).

A century earlier United States Postal Inspector Anthony Comstock raided bookstores carrying material he considered obscene. In 1873 Comstock Laws made it illegal to mail any product deemed "obscene, lewd and/or lascivious." For Comstock, these ranged from contraceptive devices and medical textbooks to the works of Voltaire and Walt Whitman. Huge public bonfires were lit to destroy the obscene material. The same Comstock Laws were in effect during the summer of 1972 – hence *Deep Throat* being distributed hand-to-hand, not by mail – but lawmakers at the time were beginning to question what was legally obscene. Hollywood itself had just replaced the restrictive Hays Code of 1930, initially started by another former United States Postal Inspector, Will H. Hays, with the Motion Picture Association of

America rating system that would eventually rank movies as G, PG, PG-13, R and NC-17. Filmmakers now had Tinseltown's blessing to explore more adult topics, which made it easier to produce films like the gigolo-centric *Midnight Cowboy* and the transgender fantasy *Myra Breckinridge*.

What was legal to publicly *show*, however, was a totally different discussion. The Supreme Court, led by Justice Earl Warren, struggled to replace Comstock's broad, vague concept of obscenity with a perspective appropriate to postwar America. "Though rarely achieving unanimity, the Warren Court progressively contracted the domain of obscenity, in large part by affirming the appropriateness of sex as a matter for public consumption... [It observed] that 'sex and obscenity are not synonymous,'" says the book *Intimate Matters: A History Of Sexuality In America*. The Supreme Court's viewpoint did not dissuade states from holding their own obscenity trials, and in 1972 *Deep Throat* cases began in several courts nationwide, including in New York. "It has ... become a symbolic target in Mayor [John] Lindsay's attempt to rid the Times Square area of commercialized sex," the *New York Times* wrote about *Deep Throat*. "The Mayor and the legitimate theater owners and other businessmen might like to wipe out the pornography industry, but it nevertheless seems to be meeting a substantial public demand." Many thousands of New Yorkers were going to Times Square's New Mature World Theater each week to catch *Deep Throat*. The audiences included "celebrities, diplomats, critics, businessmen, women alone and dating couples, few of whom, it might be presumed, would previously have gone to see a film of sexual intercourse, fellatio and cunnilingus." Newspapers printed photos of celebrity *Deep Throat* fans, including Jack Nicholson and Truman Capote. When asked his opinion of the movie, Capote said, "I thought the girl was charming."

Beneath Manhattan, telecommunications specialist Charles Dolan had spent years installing miles-long stretches of cable. The spider web of wires connected to all the major New York City hotels. Dolan's company, Teleguide, Inc., fed information to the hotels that would help them with customer service and checkout. Teleguide, Inc. expanded into Sterling Manhattan Cable, the first urban cable network in America, and caught the attention of Time-Life, Inc., which decided to buy a stake in the company. Dolan then pitched a new idea to Time-Life: a national cable channel using satellite beams, not cable wires. In 1972 Time-Life launched Home Box Office network, or HBO, the first premium programming channel. Not under the same FCC regulations or commercial constraints as ABC, CBS or NBC, Home Box Office could broadcast unedited, uninterrupted sports events, theatrical movies and original programming directly into subscribers' homes. *Midnight Blue*, a weekly cable program, showed porn clips and interviews with adult movie stars. One of the first episodes featured the cast of *Deep Throat*.

On the opposite coast, California engineers Nolan Bushnell and Ted Dabney were also convinced entertainment technology was going to be the next big thing. They pitched in $500 – two hundred and fifty bucks apiece – and began Atari, the first major American video game company. (A disputed history has Atari culling its concepts from military engineer Ralph Baer, a man who is often called "The Godfather of video games.") Atari was actually named after a move made in the Japanese strategy game Go. Bushnell had tried doing an arcade game before — 1971's *Computer Space*, released through coin-operated manufacturer Nutting Associates — but it was too complex for the average bar patron accustomed to pinball. He guessed that people would need something simpler.

Shortly after starting Atari, Bushnell hired Al Alcorn, a former associate of Dabney's, to create a table tennis video game. Two players would use their paddles to smack a brick-shaped ball back and forth. The instructions were only one sentence: "AVOID MISSING BALL FOR HIGH SCORE." They would call the black-and-white game *Pong*.

In Summer 1972 Alcorn set up a *Pong* prototype in Andy Capp's Tavern, a hole-in-the-wall bar in Sunnyvale, California. Two weeks later he got a call from the manager. The game had stopped working. Alcorn got over as soon as he could and opened up the coin box to give himself a free game. As he unlocked the machine, a cascade of quarters spilled from the box. The *Pong* arcade game stopped working because too many quarters jammed the system. In its first year there were more orders for *Pong* than any other pinball machine at the time. While other coin-operated machines brought in about fifty bucks a week, Pong often brought in two hundred dollars. Atari was still collecting quarters from its arcade route, which had grown considerably. Bushnell, a sailing aficionado, was able to buy a yacht and multiple homes.

Another entrepreneur, Reuben Sturman, distributed wooden boxes all across America and Canada. Sturman's enclosed unit, just wide and tall enough for someone to sit comfortably, had a wooden seat, a film projector and a door. The user would deposit a token, close the door, and press a button to pick one of several movie choices. An 8-mm pornographic movie would play for about a minute, maybe less. You would then have to purchase more tokens from the host up front to continue watching. Before inventing the personal peep booth, Sturman already owned, according to Hustler publisher Larry Flynt, twelve hundred adult bookstores across America. "With the peep booths, that's when my thing took off," Sturman said in an interview. "Money was coming in so fast I didn't know what to do with it. Guys come in with bags of $50,000, $100,000." Sturman would funnel money through business fronts, coerce porn shops into purchasing his products and live in several different residencies to hide his whereabouts. If he went out, he would often wear an elaborate disguise. The most public of rare Sturman photos has him wearing a large fedora hat, a business suit one size too large and black-rim glasses connected to a bulbous plastic nose and a wide, bushy mustache. (It wasn't clear if the mustache was fake, too.) Sturman had many enemies, but his most feared may have been the FBI. The agency spent more than two decades trying to smoke the incognito porn magnate out of his hole. Sturman probably took comfort when the FBI lost its obscenity-obsessed leader, J. Edgar Hoover. The seventy-seven year old FBI director died of a heart attack on May 2, 1972, three weeks before the *Deep Throat* premiere.

■ ■ ■

When considering the first fruits of motion picture technology, it is natural to think about black-and-white slapstick comedies or epic masterpieces like D. W. Griffith's racially-charged *Birth of a Nation*. Short, erotic movies, called stag films, often as brief as a mere minute, were also an important part of this initial group. It could show a couple making out, a woman fondling her breasts or a shy young lady showing a little leg.. Stag films allowed America, for the first time, to easily observe itself.

During the Second World War, the military used a machine called the radio teletype, or RTTY, to transmit text messages. Creative men and women could use the letters and symbols, comparable to those on a modern day keyboard, to make exceptional replicas of pin-ups. By the sixties computers still weren't cheap enough for the average household, but became available at major American college campuses. Dedicated nerds would spend hours in the computer lab turning their favorite Playboy centerfolds into text form, saving the images onto punch tape reels and printing them off to hang on the wall. In one of these labs MIT engineering student Steve Russell created *Spacewar*, considered the first video game ever made. The two-player spaceship battle inspired Nolan Bushnell to create games.

Before launching Atari, Bushnell was hired by Ampex Corporation, a California engineering company often credited with inventing the modern videotape. The University of Utah grad had worked as a midway barker, convincing passersby to throw baseballs at stacked milk bottles. Bushnell's job at Ampex was to work on a digital recording system, but, typical of his restless personality, he got bored within a few months. He kept thinking about *Spacewar*, the game he spent hours playing in the computer lab at his alma mater, and he knew could make money on it if he brought it to the masses. Ampex understood that engineers were happiest when doing their own experiments, so it allowed Bushnell to take spare parts home and tinker on what would become *Spacewar*, the coin operated version of *Computer Space*. Bushnell turned his two-year-old daughter's bedroom into his workshop, and he left Ampex in 1972 to start Atari.

Atari entered the home market with 1974's *Home Pong*. *Pong's* enduring popularity, along with a favorable distribution partnership with Sears Roebuck, made *Home Pong* a holiday bestseller. By 1976, the toy manufacturer Connecticut Leather Company, or Coleco, released a multi-game system (with a *Pong* clone) that cost half as much as *Home Pong*. Fairchild Camera and Instrument created the Channel F, the first video game system to have interchangeable cartridges. Atari was already working on a top-secret cartridge-based system, codenamed Stella (after a "hot-looking" employee), but it needed more capital to get the system out and, in 1976, a weak economy made going public not a viable option. In desperation, Bushnell sold Atari to Warner Communications for $28 million. He would stay on as chairman, but quickly became tired of the new corporate structure and left. (He then founded Chuck E. Cheese pizza arcades, a venture that would be worth billions.) Warner Communications invested an estimated $100 million into the once-small company, and Atari finally released the Atari 2600 VCS (Video Cartridge System) in October 1977. The 2600 had more features than the Channel F, such as selectable game difficulty, and a new game controller, a chunky brick with a button and a long pole in the middle, called a joystick. Still a considerable force in the arcade industry, Atari could do home translations of its hottest coin-op titles like *Breakout* and sell them on its 2600 system at a premium. Atari had another bestseller on its hands.

As Atari blossomed, Sony, Kodak and several other companies joined Ampex in the race to create a reliable home video system. By the mid-seventies, the competition narrowed to Sony and JVC/Panasonic and its two video cassette recorders, Betamax and VHS. Compared to VHS, Betamax had faster playback and easier queuing to find specific parts of a movie. Betamax didn't have any pornographic films, which Sony decided not to support. Home movies took off, but the inferior VHS format, not Betamax, would become the standard. As Eric Schlosser notes in his book *Reefer Madness*, "… when videocassette players became widely available to American consumers, adult film companies offered their titles on video, while the major Hollywood studios resisted the new medium. As a result, by 1979, 75 percent of all the videotapes sold in the United States were hard-core films."

■ ■ ■

In the early eighties, John Holmes was well known inside as well as outside of the porn industry. Lanky and awkward, Holmes had a thirteen-inch penis as wide as the average male wrist. Up until *Deep Throat*, Holmes and others were usually seen in short movies called loops, modern X-rated versions of stag films. The sixty-two minute *Deep Throat*, as well as *Debbie Does Dallas* and *Beyond The Green Door*, extended the length of the average porn, allowing audiences to get to know the people on the movie screen and, later, the television. The popularity of the VCR made Holmes, as well as Linda Lovelace, Vanessa Del Rio and Marilyn Chambers, pornographic film superstars. Porn companies could now sell home versions of their most popular movies. Holmes did dozens of loops for Caballero Control Corporation, a movie company that released the highly-popular Swedish Erotica series and would bring most of its theater productions to home video by the eighties. Caballero and other companies with a strong movie catalog could make millions translating them cheaply for home consumption. Between 1980 and 1983, Caballero released more than fifty Swedish Erotica home movies alone.

The Atari 2600 was also awash in entertainment options. The vintage Atari 2600 still led the pack, holding the market from new (and technically superior) systems Intellivision and Colecovision. It had the biggest user base. It had the most games. Unlike the home video market, all the video games were made by the same folks that made the hardware. Only Atari created 2600 games, which would be the equivalent of Sony being the only company making PlayStation 3 games. (Sony publishes only about twenty percent of the PS3 game library.) This absolute control allowed Atari to make money on both the system and the games, selling, as the old saying goes, both the razor and the blades. It also didn't give designers credit: the cartridge would just read "Atari."

In 1980, four game creators, wanting more credit and more creative control, left Atari and created Activision, the first third-party video game company. Its first major hit was *David Crane's Pitfall*. Atari immediately sued but could not stop Activision from making $65 million its first year developing for both the 2600 and Intellevision. Atari and Activision settled out of court and agreed that Activision could continue to make games, but only if Atari received a royalty for each 2600 title sold. This established the modern day royalty system. "People watched this case very closely because a lot of money could be made by marketing games for different systems; especially the 2600," Leonard Hermann says in *Phoenix: The Fall and Rise of Home Videogames.* "Following the lead of Activision, many other companies jumped on the bandwagon. By the summer of 1982, dozens of companies announced that they were releasing 2600 compatible games." That year Caballero Control Corporation linked with American Multiple Industries, a manufacturer of video and audio cassette storage cases, and created the Atari 2600 game company Mystique. It was named after one of Caballero's movies.

Both video game and porn producers began to realize that home audiences, not the arcade or theater audiences, were now the ones to target. Creating an arcade game could be a heavily orchestrated event with art designers, programmers and manual laborers to put together the 8 foot tall, 200 pound machine, while a home video game cartridge was usually done by one guy who did all the programming, graphics and level design.

A straight-to-video movie had a fraction of the production cost a traditional film carried, not to mention fewer distribution problems and less film crew. A hit porn could be made by two guys, a woman and a camcorder. It was no longer about translating products to the home, but making products specifically for the home. "The turning point came in 1982, when it finally went all video," pornographer Ed Deroo said in Jennifer Osborne and Legs McNeil's *The Other Hollywood*. "I missed film tremendously. Film had soul; video has nothing. Video's just a way of making money." Cabellero's Swedish Erotica compilation could go for $79.95, while Mystique's first title, *Custer's Revenge*, retailed for $49.95.

Released in 1982, *Custer's Revenge* is named after the famous general who took his last stand at Little Big Horn. "After winning a battle in 1869, Lieutenant Colonel George Armstrong Custer allegedly invited his officers to 'avail themselves of the services of a captured squaw,' while he selected a Cheyenne woman named Monasetah for himself," according to the book *Intimate Matters*. "The image of the good Indian – the beautiful, pure princess who saved white men, as did Pocahontas – gave way in the nineteenth century to the image of the savage and promiscuous squaw. Cowboy lore in particular elaborated on the theme of the Indian whore, who 'lays on her back in a cowboy shack, and lets cowboys poke her in the crack.'"

In *Custer's Revenge*, you move a pixelized cowboy from one end of the screen to the other, avoiding deadly arrows falling from the sky, to reach a submissive Native American woman tied to a cactus. If he makes it to the woman, he grabs her and has sex until, after twenty or so strokes, the next level begins and he starts over. Custer's body is pink and nude, defined by wiry appendages, a round belly and a penis as long as his arm. His only attire is brown cowboy boots, which are more wide than tall, a sky blue 10-gallon hat and a thin mauve bandanna wrapped around his neck. The bandanna flips between two opposite frames of animation, flapping flatly in the "wind."

The captive Native American woman has brown skin, thin long legs and a body like a reversed eighth note. The maiden's enormous chest points out towards Custer like an arrow over her flat stomach, and her ass protrudes nearly as much in the opposite direction. Her arms are akimbo and her mouth and eyes are wide open, as if anticipating rapture. She only wears a black headband with a dull brown feather sticking out. With an overdeveloped top, skinny legs and the wire-like feather extending from her head, she wouldn't be out of place in the movie *Ants*. The background is decorated with brown mountains that recall meatloaf and immobile white clouds above a mauve teepee, the same color as Custer's scarf, shooting chunky smoke signals. In the higher game levels green cacti, shaped like the number 4, are placed randomly in the foreground and must be avoided to reach the maiden. According to the game box cover, the Native American woman herself is tied to a tall, straight cactus, but graphic limitations put her game character in front of the cactus, hands behind her. If Custer reaches the woman, he immediately lifts her up, puts her legs straight against his hip, and begins having sex. The animation jumps between two jerky frames, flotsam and jetsam. His hands are on her protruding nipples, not supporting her behind, the balance of her body weight on his long penis. The *Custer's Revenge* instruction manual was broken down into sections like Foreplay (the object of the game), Game Play and After Play (a message from the company). Another section, Scoring, says what to do when you get to the maiden. "When Custer successfully reaches the maiden, repeatedly depress the 'fire' button. Do not hold it down. You receive one point for each time you 'score'. So press it over and over again as rapidly as you can. Watch how the maiden smiles and kicks up her heels and Custer 'flips his lid'. As Custer 'scores' a fanfare of Charge is played. You do not have to wait for the tune to finish to 'score' again. Just keep pressing the button over and over again."

Mystique announced *Custer's Revenge* in October 1982, setting up a preview for retailers and the press the same week in Manhattan. Two-hundred and fifty protesters picketed in front of the New York Hilton. "The game features an enactment of a white male, General Custer, ravishing an Indian Woman who is tied to a post," Women Against Pornography member Kristen Reilly complained to the press. Her colleagues carried signs that said "*Custer's Revenge* Says Rape Is Fun" and "Stop Making Fun Out of Woman's Pain". "Once there was a lot of furor over the game, the company denied that it was rape. They claimed that it was mutually consenting visual images, which is really asinine."

By the end of the week, Atari sued Mystique and American Multiple Industries for distributing sex-themed material on its 2600 system. "Atari, like the general public, is outraged by this conduct and we are taking the initiative by filing this suit," Michael Moone, president of Atari's consumer electronics division, told the Associated Press. Atari's official comment was it "does not condone or approve this use of its home video game technology, which was designed for wholesome family entertainment." Based on the Activision court case, third-party companies didn't have to get Atari's content approval – only give a royalty on each game sold. Atari had no real power. American Multiple Industries sued Suffolk County, New York for $11 million for trying to prohibit the game from being sold. The county said the ban was legitimate since it believed *Custer's Revenge* was a danger to the health and safety of Suffolk County residents. In Canada, custom authorities approved *Custer's Revenge* for importation after its October release, but within weeks twenty groups protested. By December 1, Canadian customs reversed the decision.

As veteran video game journalist Arnie Katz recalls in the book *The Ultimate History of Video Games*, "I remember talking to a representative of [Women Against Pornography] and telling her that in my opinion, the best way to keep the game from selling was to ignore it. These were games that most people wouldn't touch with a ten-foot pole. They trained all their energy on *Custer's Revenge* and they succeeded in helping it sell twice as many copies as the other adult games." It sold eighty thousand copies at fifty bucks a pop.

Mystique released two follow-up games, *Bachelor Party* and *Beat 'Em & Eat 'Em*. *Bachelor Party* is a clone of Atari's *Breakout*. In *Breakout*, you use a bat to hit a ball against colored bricks, sort of a one-player version of *Pong*. In *Bachelor Party*, the bricks are women built like Amazons and the ball resembles a well-endowed midget. *Beat 'Em & Eat 'Em* is a variant of Activision's *Kaboom!*. In Activision's title you catch dropping bombs before they reach the bottom of the screen. In Mystique's game, you control a busty, nude blonde with her mouth wide open to the sky. A man with a penis longer than his torso drops his love down for the woman to catch. The game box, which features a cartoon of a woman licking ice cream, reads "You are a local leading-lady and all the up-town boys are standing in line for a date, but a savvy soda-slinger just around the corner is more down your alley and you just can't seem to get enough of his famous fountain treats." These games would also sell for $49.95, about twenty dollars higher than the average 2600 game.

Alan Roberts, another transplant from the porn industry, started the company Universal Game-X after directing the hit *Young Lady Chatterley*. The first game, 1983's *X-Man*, was a *Pac-Man*-inspired title with random mazes. A small pale guy with a penis the size of his legs, X-Man runs towards a door at the center of the screen while avoiding scissors, teeth and crabs, the Freudian parallel to castration, oral sex and venereal diseases. The game changes once you make it to the door. Two huge, block characters appear: X-Man, standing in the buff, and a blonde with purple skin bent over in front of him. X-Man's long penis is in the purple woman's behind. Now you must get the right rhythm, moving the joystick left and right, to make the woman come. (It would be the first time in console game history the goal was to pleasure the woman.) Her nipples enlarge based on your performance. A whirly, flute-like sound effect repeats faster as she gets closer to coming. When the round ends, points are tallied based on the number of orgasms achieved. "The response from players has been enthusiastic – women and men. We were anticipating terrific business, but it has been hindered as a result of the Mystique line and the bad press that came from it," Roberts said in a magazine interview at the time. "Certain stores think that because *Custer* was a bad game, all adult games are bad games. That's not true at all." *X-Man* flopped, sinking Universal Game-X shortly after its release. As the *Custer's Revenge* controversy died down, Mystique also experienced a drop in sales. *Custer's Revenge* was the only title not based on another popular game, and sales of *Bachelor Party* and *Beat 'Em & Eat 'Em* were relatively poor. Caballero Control Corporation closed Mystique. Alan Roberts went back to movies, directing *Young Lady Chatterley II* and *The Happy Hooker Goes To Hollywood*.

The rights to *Custer's Revenge* and the other Mystique games were sold to Game Source, a California-based company. Under the moniker Playaround, Game Source re-released *Custer's Revenge*, *Beat 'Em & Eat 'Em* and *Bachelor Party* with two key differences. Playaround created what it called the "double ender," a two-in-one cartridge that sounded like it was a two-headed dildo. Playaround's long cartridges allowed players to buy two of its games for one low price, a marketing ploy imitated by other companies. Playaround also created female versions of the Mystique games, the first time that sexual games were made for women. *Bachelor Party* became *Bachelorette Party*, *Beat 'Em & Eat 'Em* became *Philly Flasher* (replacing cumshots with breast milk), and *Custer's Revenge* was renamed *Westward Ho*. Playaround simply modified the titles and switched the main characters from male to female. New games were the medieval romp *Lady In Waiting/Knight On The Town*, the maze title *Gigolo/Cathouse Blues* and the flying game *Jungle Fever/ Burning Desire*. (The latter wasn't another game about interracial sex.) Similar to Mystique, all of Playaround's new games were clones of its competitors' titles. Demand for Playaround's games weren't enough to encourage stores to carry its products, so gamers who actually wanted *Philly Flasher* could rarely find it at the store. Playaround closed shop as quickly as it opened.

Toy stores shelves sagged under the weight of the hundreds of Atari 2600 games being released every year. Atari's open market system offered no checks and balances. *The Kool-Aid Man* had a game, as did the movie *Porky's*. Atari itself shipped an estimated four million copies of *Pac-Man*, even though there were only 10 million Atari 2600 owners. Milton Bradley, Quaker Oats and countless other companies jumped into the industry, often with their own systems, dividing the flagging video game market even further. Overstocked and underselling, Toys 'R' Us and other retailers began having bargain bins filled with five dollar titles that were $29.95 a week earlier. Those that invested the most in the video game business ended 1983 in debt. Coleco posted record losses for its fifty year history. Atari lost $583 million in one year.

As the year closed Catherine MacKinnon and Andrea Dworkin, two feminist theorists against pornography, organized a Minneapolis City Council meeting called the "Public Hearings on Ordinance to Add Pornography as Discrimination Against Women." It consisted of testimony from women who felt their lives were destroyed by pornography.

One participant, a woman who went by "Ms. U." for anonymity purposes, discussed her sexual assault. "I was attacked by two white men. From the beginning they let me know they hated my people, even though it was obvious from their remarks that they knew very little about us. And they let me know that the rape of a 'squaw' by white men was practically honored by white society. In fact, it has been made into a video game called Custer's [Revenge]. And that's what they screamed in my face as they threw me to the ground, 'This is more fun than Custer's [Revenge]!' They held me down, and as one was running the tip of the knife across my face and throat, he said, 'Do you want to play Custer's [Revenge]? It's great. You lose, but you don't care, do you? You like a little pain, don't you, squaw?' They both laughed and then he said, 'There is a lot of cock in Custer's [Revenge]. You should be grateful, squaw, that all-American boys like us want you. Maybe we will tie you to a tree and start a fire around you.'"

Defending Custer's Revenge the year before, American Multiple Industries President Stuart Kesten explained why AMI and Mystique made the game. "We just couldn't see adults playing with spaceships anymore."

# PROTECTION

The White House Press Secretary seems confused, though he's the one holding court on this October 1982 day. A reporter asks Press Secretary Larry Speakes, "Does the President have any reaction to the announcement the Centers for Disease Control in Atlanta has that AIDS is now an epidemic and has over 600 cases?" "What's AIDS," Speakes asks. "Over a third of them have died. It's known as 'gay plague'…" the reporter says. The group laughs. "No, it is. I mean, it's a pretty serious thing that one in every three people that gets this has died. And I wondered if the President is aware of it?" "I don't have it," Speakes says. "Do you?" Laughter fills the room and the question disappears into oblivion.

"634 Americans had been stricken with AIDS by October 5, 1982. Of these, 260 were dead," Randy Shilts later wrote in *And The Band Played On*. "There was no rush to spend money, mobilize public health officials, or issue regulations that might save lives." Four years later, President Ronald Reagan would go on live TV to discuss the so-called gay plague. Addressing Congress about the disease now known as Acquired Immune Deficiency Syndrome, he said, "An unprecedented research effort is underway to deal with this major epidemic public health threat." Based on the research of the French Institut Pasteur and, later, the National Cancer Institute, citizens learned AIDS was a blood-based disease transmitted through sharing needles, blood transfusions and oral, vaginal and anal sex. Nearly everyone who was sexually active was at risk. Some Christian conservatives looked at AIDS as a holy backlash to the open-minded sex culture of the seventies. "AIDS is not just God's punishment for homosexuals," said Pastor Jerry Falwell. "It is God's punishment for the society that tolerates homosexuals." A popular, later parodied commercial suggested that if you sleep with a woman, you're also sleeping with her previous partners, and her partners' previous partners, "and so on, and so on…" and the television screen would fill up with faces in squares like a *The Brady Bunch* credit sequence gone mad. "In the 1960s, when the birth control pill and IUD became readily available, the condom was practically rendered obsolete. Good girls just did it, and penicillin prevailed," notes "Sexpert" Dr. Ava Candell. "It wasn't until the AIDS epidemic in the 1980s that condom use regained its prominence." A report in the American Journal of Public Health found that condom sales rose from 240 million in 1986 to nearly 300 million in 1988, the biggest jump happening after Surgeon General C. Everett Koop's 1987 report on AIDS. Trojan, Durex and other manufacturers used machines, robotic arms and detached metal phalli, to stretch test condoms for durability and leaks.

New technology allowed people to connect physically as well as by the bits and bytes in the computer. Richard Bartle and Roy Trubshaw, two University of Essex students, created a computer program called *Multi-User Dungeon, or MUD*. A text-only adventure, *MUD* would give you a description of the room you are in, the objects in it and the fellow players around. The British undergrads were inspired by *Dungeons & Dragons*, the American pen-and-paper fantasy game where players would go on elaborate journeys. In *D & D*, an appointed leader, called the Dungeon Master, would establish the rules and direct the heroes. Bartle and Trubshaw wanted the Dungeon Masters to be *MUD* players, too. Thousands of individual gamers used their university computers to play together, sometimes calling or even traveling to meet each other in person. One player, Sue the Witch, became one of the most popular *MUD* adventurers, spending up to six hours online a night and racking up a 1,000 British pound phone bill every month. She also stood out as one of the few female players. Despite requests and her obvious commitment to the game, Sue refused to meet with others. She said she was agoraphobic, but would mail pictures of herself and talk with her *MUD* friends on the phone. One day, Sue sent a terse message saying that she was going to take a break for a while. According to the book *Dungeons and Dreamers*, a group of players discovered Sue's address in England and decided to surprise her with a visit. "A woman answered their knock at the door and gave them the bad news: Sue's real name was actually Steve. He'd been playing as a woman since the beginning, letting his wife – whose real name was Sue – answer the phone calls." Steve announced his break just before he was sent away to prison for defrauding a government agency.

Another *MUD* alumnus, Neil Newell, created the computer game *Shades*. Newell wanted a world larger than *MUD*. (*Shades* would have more than 500 rooms.) He also wanted players to have privacy. In *MUD* and other games, the "admin," short for administrator, would be privy to every action. Confide with an online friend about your marriage problems and the admin would hear the whole conversation. For *Shades*, Newell made "safe areas"—neutral zones where there would be no fighting and complete privacy for the people inside. "I'd say the 'cybersex' emerged on *Shades* simply because it was the first game that gave players a guaranteed private area," Newell says in *Sex in Video Games*. "Naively, I figured people were hanging out in the safe areas for private chats. Cybering [hooking up with people online] wasn't a well-known phenomenon back then." There were other channels for intimate conversations. Bulletin Board Systems, or BBSs, allowed users to have private chats. You'd call a certain number with your computer modem and exchange messages, not unlike an early form of email. (You could also download files, which made BBSs a precursor to Internet pornography.) Since it was a game, *Shades* was more user-friendly than the average BBS. It was one of the first titles, if not the first title to allow cyber sex within its boundaries. Journalist Julian Dibbell later discussed the unique MUD dynamics in his Village Voice article *A Rape In Cyberspace*, observing player's reactions to a virtual public sexual assault in the game *LambdaMOO*. "And then there were what I'll call the techno-libertarians. For them, MUD rapists were of course assholes, but the presence of assholes on the system was a technical inevitability, like noise on a phone line…" Like *MUD* and *Shades*, *LambdaMOO* was a text-only game.

Game players and programmers had to have university connections to use expensive computers, but advances in technology brought systems like the Apple ][, the IBM PC and the Atari 800 into people's homes. Two thousand dollars got you a computer almost as powerful as yesterday's bulky university mainframe. Unlike the Atari 2600 and other video game consoles, you could tell the computer what to do: learn a programming language and teach it to do a balance spreadsheet, play a musical note or display a picture. It also democratized who could make games, the equivalent of affordable camcorders unleashing more independent filmmakers. For instance, a teenager named Richard Garriott programmed a homemade adventure game, *Akalabeth: World of Doom*, stuffed copies into Ziploc bags and sold them, with the help of a small local distributor, to other Apple ][ users. In the first year he made $150,000. He started Origin, one of the first major computer game companies, and later sold it to Electronic Arts for thirty million dollars. Origin was one of several small gaming companies that would become heavyweights in the future.

Another game creator, IBM engineer Arthur Walsh, learned programming when his manager started writing for the popular computer magazine *Byte*. Walsh tried teaching his computer to play bridge. It worked, and the success got Walsh hooked on making games. Wanting to one-up Walsh, his supervisor decided to make a flight simulator, which also became a decent game. After a few homemade projects, the two employees decided to leave IBM and start a game company. Walsh had been with IBM for more than twenty five years. Shortly after leaving, the two colleagues had a disagreement over the direction of the company and Walsh decided to start his own venture, Artworx. The new three person team acquired a few different Atari 800 games, including Walsh's bridge title and a solid, but somewhat boring poker game programmed by an outside contractor. "There were more poker players than bridge players out there, so we thought 'Why don't we push poker?' One of my associates said, making a joke, 'I bet if it was strip poker, it would sell.' I was like 'You're right! Why can't we do that?' That was the birth of the idea," Walsh said in an interview. He decided *Strip Poker: A Sizzling Game of Chance* wasn't going to be an erotic game, but instead feature funny cartoon-inspired characters so it wouldn't offend purchasers of other Artworx software. The company artist, however, vehemently disagreed, as did the third employee, and convinced Walsh that they should make the game as realistic as possible. The Atari 800 had a resolution of 320 pixels across x 192 pixels down, less than half of the pocket sized iPod Nano, and was capable of four colors at a time. Artworx's artist would obtain real photographs, develop them onto slides and project them onto the outside of the computer monitor. The third employee created a drawing program especially for *Strip Poker*. Guided by the slides, they would copy each image into the game pixel by pixel. The one aspect Artworx didn't handle was the photography itself, which was done by an outside contractor. "Our photographer wasn't a fashion one, but he was good at photographic women. He would find a good place, a hotel or something, and take pictures of them in the bed or in the bathroom. Later he would make sure the hotel had a Jacuzzi, because in the final nude scene, the 'modesty scene' we call it, the woman would be completely nude except for some bubbles," Walsh said.

In the final game, the background would be pitch black and opponents would lay horizontally, from left to right, as if sprawled atop a fireplace-warmed bearskin rug. One woman would wear thigh-hugging hot pants and a low-cut polo shirt, her long, blonde tresses tumbling past her ample cleavage. The four opponents would have six different poses – the number of successful poker hands it takes to get to a modesty scene – and three different outfits chosen at random. Artworx also sold expansion packs, called "data disks," that added twenty-four opponents. Two of them were male. "It was probably radical at the time," Walsh said. "We had women on staff, so I talked to them when we were developing this to see what they thought of [having male opponents], but from an appearance standpoint it was important: We wanted to be even handed. And obviously, if there was a demand, we would appeal to the demand."

*Strip Poker: A Sizzling Game of Chance* was released on the Atari 800 in 1982. "The Atari version became quite popular. Then it went to Apple, then the original PC when it came out," Walsh said. "As far as competition, anytime you've got something that sells, other companies will say 'We can do it, too.'" Clones included *Cover Girl Poker* and *Samantha Fox Strip Poker*, the latter featuring the popular adult film star, but the competition forced Artworx to take risks. "In order to make use of the photos, we would have the player go against both a male and female opponent in the same game. We also did it with two women at the same time," Walsh said, adding "The multi-opponent ones were very popular. But we've also seen it be used by a spouse – a husband will use it as an excuse to buy it because he's 'buying it for his wife.'"

■ ■ ■

Just prior to *Strip Poker* hitting the shelves, *Time* magazine featured an article on On-Line Systems, a small company run by husband-and-wife team Ken and Roberta Williams, and its adult text game, *Softporn Adventure*. "On-line, a California software company, sells a program called Softporn for $29.25. In the computer fantasy game, players seek to seduce three women, while avoiding hazards, such as getting killed by a bouncer in a disco." *Time* actually showed the box art along with the article. It features three nude women in an outdoor Jacuzzi, the bubbling hot water rising just high enough to cover their nipples. They are sipping from champagne glasses, and a waiter with a jet-black helmet of hair stands awkwardly behind them. In the background, next to the waiter, partially obscured by the second woman's hairdo, is the Apple ][. On-line Systems had done a big advertising campaign in major computer magazines like *Softalk*, using the unchanged box art as the ad. "I got a copy of *Softporn* as soon as I got my Apple ][. Hell, everyone had a copy of *Softporn*! You'd think it was packaged with the Apple ][," said eighties game designer Al Lowe. Lowe would soon be working for the nude woman in the far right of the *Softporn* ad. The blonde with the baby face was On-Line Systems co-owner Roberta Williams.

Lowe began programming when he bought his first home computer, an Apple ][ with 48K RAM, a 9" green screen, two 120K floppy drives and a state-of-the-art Epson MX80 printer ($3,500). A music teacher, Lowe convinced himself the computer would help him with work, even creating a simple program to organize his class schedules, but he really got the system so he and his son could play together. The first games he bought were the adventure *Cranston Manor* and the *Pac-Man* clone *Gobbler*, both by On-line Systems. Lowe became more serious about the Apple ][ when he went to a music convention and stayed around for a computer convention. "The music convention had been pretty much the same old stuff I'd known and seen – kind of all the same things over again – whereas the next week's show was so exciting and so full of new technology," Lowe said. He happened to mention his homemade schedule program to one of the vendors. The publisher offered him a deal. Lowe went back home and perfected the program – just in time for the publisher to go out of business. In a last-ditch effort, Lowe and his wife went to AppleFest '82, a popular conference that summer, and purchased a 10' x 10' booth with a month's income (combined). "I'm there, and down the hall comes [On-line Systems co-owner] Ken Williams, and as usual he was antsy, walking around the booths to see what was new. And he gets to our booth, stops, and yells 'Hey 'berta! These games look just like yours!'" Ken and Roberta were impressed by the software and asked them to come by the On-line Systems booth first thing in the morning to talk about a publishing deal: Lowe would make the software, On-Line would distribute it. Within a year Lowe quit teaching music and become a full-time game designer for On-line Systems. The up-and-coming company moved to a mountainous region of California and renamed itself Sierra On-Line.

When Lowe came aboard, Sierra On-Line had just successfully negotiated the use of Disney characters in their games – provided it drop the best-selling *Softporn Adventure* from its catalog. Lowe became instrumental in bringing the wholesome characters to the Apple ][, creating graphics, music and level design to products like *Donald Duck's Playground* and *Winnie the Pooh in the 100-Acre Woods*. Sierra On-Line had also invested a significant amount of money into developing Atari 2600 software and, as a result of the 1983 video game crash, ended up laying off two-thirds of its staff. Ken Williams asked Lowe to leave his full-time programmer post to become a consultant, a work-for-hire employee who would be paid an advance upfront against royalties for each product he was involved in. "He shows me the advance and it's like double the money I was making before! So I say yes. And then, as I stared to walk away, I ask 'Have I just been fired?' Ken says, 'Yes.' I say, 'Oh, OK.' I remained an outside contractor for the next fifteen years." Not unlike Disney's standard employee contract, Lowe's new agreement meant that he wouldn't have much, if any say as to how his characters or creations were used. Any requested feedback would be a courtesy.

Sierra On-Line's Disney licensed expired in 1986. Ken Williams recommended the company look at updating *Softporn Adventure*, the 1981 title that sold approximately 25,000 copies at a time when there were only 100,000 Apple ][s. Lowe excitedly went home, dusted off his Apple ][ and played the game. "I was appalled. It was literally a game about a guy getting laid… It had no protagonist, little or no plot, almost no text, understood almost no input. So I reported back to Ken: there's no way I could bring this game into the eighties unless he let me make fun of that lifestyle. I said 'It's so behind the times it might as well be wearing a leisure suit!' And everyone laughed… Thus was born *Leisure Suit Larry*."

Lowe was in his late thirties, happily married to his wife, Margaret. The two music teachers had a son and daughter, Brian and Megan, who would both end up happily married as well. Lowe had never been to a strip club. "Larry is the anti-Al," he admitted later. "There's not much of Larry in me. That's why I could make fun of him in the game. It was sincere." Lowe determined that Larry would be a 30-year-old loser wandering the streets of "Los Wages," equipped with only a permanent erection. Wearing a tight white suit with a butterfly collar, Larry represented an era of key parties, unprotected sex and orgy-friendly bathhouses. Larry was a living relic.

Lowe didn't think much of *Softporn Adventure*, with its lack of storyline and narrow scope, but the puzzles, the puzzles in *Softporn* were smart, very old school. It reminded him of the late '70s text adventures like Scott Adams' *Adventure* or Willie Crowther's seminal *Colossal Cave*, games with thoughtful, occasionally frustrating situations, but puzzles that were always solvable and often brilliant in hindsight. Like the beginning of *Softporn Adventure*, Larry would start in front of a dive bar called Lefty's. There would be no instructions on what to do next. Making any type of progress in the game required unconventional forethought. For instance, when you receive a cocktail from Lefty's grimy bartender, your first instinct is to drink it. Instead, if you take the drink and give it to the homeless man laying in the bar's back alley, he'll tell you the secret password to enter a neighboring speakeasy where a lady (and her pimp) is waiting for you. If players outsmarted the game – outsmarted Lowe – they would be rewarded with sex. (Lowe even managed to turn sex into a puzzle: in one case, Larry will die if he has sex without using a condom found in a previous area.) The actual act was more implied than explicit: when Larry does finally get laid, the naked scene is covered with a big, black CENSORED! bar that moves and stretched around the couple like an accordion. "Every adventure game was swords and sandals or save the galaxy from these aliens. I thought 'I can't do another space game. I can't do another king's quest game.' I wanted something the average guy can relate to," Lowe said.

Lowe spent Winter 1986 working from home, dedicating his time to perfecting *Leisure Suit Larry*'s in-game puzzles. If he found one hilarious, he would often redo the puzzle to make it funnier. After months of revisions Lowe posted a notice on Compuserve, one of the first online service providers. Lowe said that he and Ken Williams were looking for ten people to test the new Sierra game for bugs and, more importantly, humor. The response was overwhelming, and it also was the first documented time a game company did an official public beta-testing. "I did it because I wanted the game to understand as much as it could," Lowe said. Each beta-test copy of *Leisure Suit Larry* had a special file. The program would make a note whenever the player typed in a command it didn't understand. "I would go, 'Oh, somebody typed that? Oh, OK.' I would then create an in-game response to that, or create a new puzzle." Each typed command, such as "open door" or "have sex," needed to be programmed in. In his sex game, Lowe would have to anticipate everything that the gamer could possibly want to do.

Sierra released two new adventure games in the summer of 1987: *Leisure Suit Larry in the Land of the Lounge Lizards* and the gritty Dirty Harry-inspired cop adventure *Police Quest: In Pursuit of the Death Angel*. Games were usually sold hand-to-hand by eager salespeople, by word of mouth and by the cover art and text. *Softporn Adventure* ads notwithstanding, video game advertisements were still in relative infancy. Two decades later *Grand Theft Auto III* and other gamers supported by Hollywood-sized budgets would have commercial spots during *The Tonight Show*. In 1987, computer games sales methods weren't much different than the Ziploc days. As a result, games that seemed the most familiar were generally the best sellers. Sierra's other top titles, *King's Quest III: To Heir is Human* and *Space Quest II: Vohaul's Revenge*, were already part of their respective well-established series. *Police Quest* was new, but it carried the "Quest" moniker and had a stylish cover reminiscent of a Clint Eastwood movie. (Eastwood's next Dirty Harry movie, *The Dead Pool*, would be out the upcoming summer.) The cover of *Leisure Suit Larry* had the hero with his pickle nose, oversized head and butterfly-collared shirt, sipping a martini and leaning against a TV displaying a naked digital woman in a Jacuzzi, reminiscent of the *Softporn* ad.

Overseas, Palace Software released the action game *Barbarian: The Ultimate Warrior*. On the cover was a warrior couple played by an unknown male model and Maria Whittaker, a busty "page 3 girl." An iconic feature, British tabloids often featured a nude or topless woman on page three. On the game box, Whittaker had a leather bikini bra, a metallic-looking thong and very long sword. "Maria Whittaker was a famous page 3 girl who had often been featured on page 3, but when she appeared on the game's cover, clad in far more clothes than usual, with a fancy brassiere and (admittedly) skimpy thong, a right to-do ensued," according to the book *High Score: The Illustrated History of Electronic Games*. "There was much protest and hoopla over the buxom Ms. Whittaker's state of dress on the *Barbarian* cover, and – this is the ironic part – nothing about the extreme gory violence of the game, which was far more gruesome than just about anything that had been previously released." Unlike *Softporn Adventure*, games like *Barbarian*, *Strip Poker* and *Leisure Suit Larry* were being sold at major electronics outlets to mainstream audiences, not directly from small home offices to techies.

"*Strip Poker* was being taken off the shelves, which was in the late eighties through the early nineties," said Artworx's Arthur Walsh. "At Electronics Boutique we had one of its best-selling programs, but we were notified that it wasn't going to buy any more of our programs. This letter was from the new Vice President of Purchasing, who said it was inappropriate for sale." Sierra was in a similar quandary when Radio Shack and several other outlets refused to carry *Leisure Suit Larry*. "*Police Quest* and *Larry* shipped. *Police Quest* flew out of the stores, but *Larry* sold, like, 4,000 copies the first month it was out. Now this is back when almost all Sierra titles sold 50,000 copies or more per month," Lowe said. It was one of the worst, if not the worst selling game in Sierra's history. Six months of hard work gone, Lowe just immersed himself in other titles, including the next *Larry* game, *Leisure Suit Larry Goes Looking for Love (in Several Wrong Places.)*. "Did my life change after *Larry* first came out? Not really," Lowe said. "My wife and I had the opinion that the game thing was kind of temporary, so she kept working as a music coordinator. We lived off of her salary."

■ ■ ■

On Monday, October 19, 1987, the New York Stock Exchange dropped more than 500 points, the equivalent of $500 billion disappearing in one day. It was the worst devaluation in American stock market history. The market was the victim of inflated Initial Public Offerings and over-hyped companies. Donald Trump revitalized Atlantic City, becoming a billionaire and, perhaps more importantly, showing that anyone could have The American Dream if they were hungry enough. *Trump: The Art of the Deal* was the number one book by the end of the year. Oliver Stone released *Wall Street*, which popularized the 1987 mantra, "Greed is good." There were enough aggressive, financially-minded high rollers around to create a new term: "yuppie," or "Young Urban Professional." Buying stock in new, future-minded companies was considered a great, fast way to get a good return on investment. Many of these new, future-minded companies were filled with hot air. They popped on Black Monday. Newspapers reported seeing broke twenty-something Manhattan penthouse owners, their Italian shoes halfway off the window ledge, yelling to the world that they were going to jump. Bobby McFerrin's video to his hit "Don't Worry, Be Happy" parodied the stock market suicides. Investors who wanted to continue to work could not – the world markets were paralyzed by the New York Stock Exchange crash.

A Wall Street employee, perhaps a bored analyst, perhaps a frustrated broker, uploaded a copy of *Leisure Suit Larry in the Land of the Lounge Lizards* onto the company's computer server. Several sources claim it was at Merrill Lynch. The managers noticed the company's computers were running sluggishly, but other firms had caught on by then. It was too late. "Computer games have proved increasing popular since the fall in trading volumes experience after the crash of October [and] dealers have filled in their work hours by playing games," said a London *Financial Times* article. "The adventures of Larry the Lounge Lizard... have proved particularly popular because of their salacious content." Those 4,000 copies *Leisure Suit Larry* sold the first month became 8,000 the next month, and 16,000 the next. By February, the Softsell Top 10 computer game chart was owned by *King's Quest 3*, *Police Quest* and *Leisure Suit Larry*. Lowe had a hand in all of them. *Leisure Suit Larry* alone would sell more than 300,000 copies.

Lowe received a call from Gruber-Peters productions, the company behind the hit Fox comedy *Married ... with Children*. It wanted to do a *Larry* sitcom. Lowe went down to their offices and set up *Leisure Suit Larry* in one of the boardrooms. About twenty employees crammed into the room to watch Lowe manipulate Larry on the 36-inch computer monitor. "So they would say something, I'd paraphrase it and type it in, and it would mostly work. Like we went into the bar, went to the bathroom to the urinals, and someone would say 'Take a leak.' I'd type it in and it worked," Lowe recalled. "Then some guy said 'Masturbate!' Now I'm thinking, I'm not sure if it'll understand – I can't remember if I programmed that in or not! So I type it in and it came back and said 'The whole idea was for you to STOP doing that!' Everyone cracked up." Other studios approached Lowe about doing a Larry movie, going as far as reading some potential scripts. "One wanted to get Jim Carrey," Lowe would later say. "He was hot from *Dumb and Dumber.*" He says studios offered horrible scripts, and those that had decent ideas wouldn't allow him to play a role in the final product. He says he was offered a considerable amount of money. He turned everything down, wanting to protect his lovable character. Shortly after *Leisure Suit Larry* shipped, a friend overseas told Lowe his game was a hit in Russia. The problem was Sierra didn't do a Russian version of the game. He later saw it himself. "I found one in Moscow for two dollars. And their CD art was even better than ours! Now, the entire game had been copied, but they couldn't figure out the audio files, so they had rerecorded the voices in Russian overdubbed it. My first reaction was 'We should hire this guy!'" Lowe's character was becoming an international icon, whether he wanted Larry to be or not.

Lowe initially saw the *Leisure Suit Larry* series as a trilogy. In *Leisure Suit Larry 3: Passionate Patti in Pursuit of the Pulsating Pectorals*, Larry finally finds his soulmate, Patti (a heroine you can control during certain segments of the game), and ends up falling out onto the "back lot" of Sierra Productions – a homage to Lowe's favorite comedy, Mel Brooks' *Blazing Saddles*. The game finishes with Larry getting hired by Ken Williams to do a new game for Sierra. "I think I'll start the game in Lost Wages, outside a bar named Lefty's," Larry says, typing the beginning of the first *Leisure Suit Larry*. Lowe publicly said there would never be a *Larry 4*. This was before *Leisure Suit Larry 3* became the most successful *Larry* game yet, and before it became obvious that Larry wasn't going to go away. Lowe and Ken Williams had another one of their talks and decided that instead of breaking up the trilogy, Sierra would put Larry online. It would be called *Larryland*. "We had this room full of modems... we thought it had to be one modem per computer," Lowe said. "With the limited bandwidth we could create a multiplayer game like chess and checkers, but we wanted to do an adventure." There was no nationwide digital infrastructure, like broadband or cable hookups, that could quickly transfer information from computer to computer to make a complex game playable. Two Sierra employees, Jeff Stephenson and Matthew George, handled the technical end. "[And] my job? Simple. All I had to do was... design the first interactive, multi-player, on-line adventure game," Lowe recalled on his online diary, *AlLowe.com*. "Needless to say, I failed." Lowe quit *LarryLand* after six difficult months. The infrastructure would eventually become The Sierra Network, an online gaming community that would struggle to make a profit in upcoming years.

Shortly after *LarryLand* failed, the company Quantum launched a sophisticated BBS program for the Macintosh. Unlike its competitors, Quantum wanted to provide Internet access and services to people new to computers. The dominant company at the time, CompuServe, was made by techies for techies. (For example, CompuServe email addresses were composed of assigned, seemingly random numbers and letters.) The Quantum service would have easy-to-use chat rooms, colorful graphics and online games. The company already had some success with its previous BBS program, Quantum Link, for the Commodore line of computers. Quantum would release the Mac version under a new name, America OnLine. In a few years it would surpass CompuServe, Prodigy and other service providers. AOL would eventually purchase The Sierra Network, shutting it down shortly after.

Despite the *LarryLand* setback, fans continued to ask Lowe when *Leisure Suit Larry* was coming back. "Are you still working on *Larry 4*?" a co-worker asked him one day. "No," he says. "I'm working on *Larry 5*." He pauses after his wise-ass comment and realizes he's onto something. Lowe began work on *Leisure Suit Larry 5: Passionate Patti Does a Little Undercover Work*, which would also go on to sell 300,000 copies. The sequel makes references to events that happened in *Larry 4* – game events that, of course, never occurred.

# OTAKU

Tokyo has many towers. There is one specific building, Tokyo Tower, which is a replica of Paris' Eiffel Tower. Created in 1958 to symbolize Japan's postwar growth, the tower cost nearly 3 billion yen and was painted burnt orange and eggshell white. It is also a few inches taller than Gustave Eiffel's original tower. Tokyo is filled with towers and, together, they create a startling skyline. Individually they are mostly unexceptional, mundane buildings that sell commonplace goods like groceries, electronics and books. In *Japan Unbound*, John Nathan explains why modern day Tokyo grows tall, not out. "In 1986 the value of Tokyo real estate doubled, and doubled again in 1987; in September of that year, one hundred square feet on the downtown Ginza was selling for $1 million. By mid-1988, the value of Japanese real estate would be worth five times that of the United States." Seven story high buildings are not unusual. You explore one floor, which is the size of a decent American kitchen, climb the thin steps, pardoning your way through the ever-present crowds, and begin exploring the next floor. While towers house everything from clothing boutiques to posh eateries, a notable amount are packed with porn. Big breast porn. Black man porn. Animal porn. Bodily function porn. Blonde porn. School girl porn. Store product is almost always well organized, sectioned off and clearly labeled on small shelves. There is usually a separate rack up front dedicated to pornographic video games. Adult stores generally focus on magazines and movies, not games, but fans of interactive porn wouldn't go to a tower of porn to get their games anyway. "From the time I arrived there, I remember the only mainstream PC games being sold in shops were on one rack, like the PC translation of Final Fantasy VII or Diablo, and the other 90 percent were sex games" said Chris Kohler, author of *Power-Up: How Japanese Video Games Gave the World an Extra Life*. "They started making erotic games pretty much as soon as they figured out how to make games."

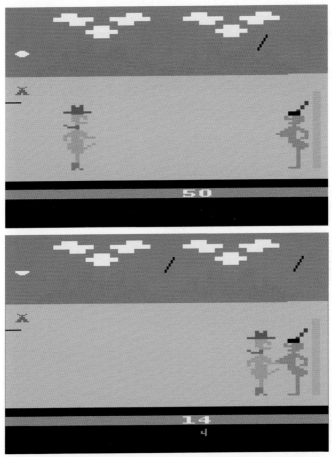

*Custer's Revenge* (Mystique, 1982) for the Atari 2600 was the first mainstream porn video game. It caused multiple protests.

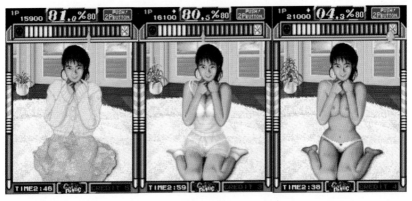

The Japanese arcade game *Gal's Panic* (Kaneko, 1990) was a top ten hit in America.

*Leisure Suit Larry: Magna Cum Laude* (Sierra, 2004) was the critically panned return of the '80s sex game icon.

The first video game to feature a lesbian couple *Fear Effect 2: Retro Helix* (Eidos, 2001) had its controversial ads banned in America.

*Dead or Alive 2* (Tecmo, 2000) was a well designed brawler, but its bouncing breasts made it infamous.

The "Hot Coffee" minigame in *Grand Theft Auto: San Andreas* (Rockstar, 2004) drew ire from Senator Hillary Rodham Clinton.

The fighter *Dead or Alive Ultimate* (Tecmo, 2004) featured more skin than its predecessors.

Despite having topless riders and strip club footage, *BMX XXX* (Acclaim, 2003) was a flop.

Ayane battles in different outfits in the fighting game *Dead or Alive Ultimate* (Tecmo, 2004).

Rachel is the heroine in *Ninja Gaiden Sigma* (Tecmo, 2007). It was designed by Tomonobu Itagaki, the man behind *Dead or Alive*.

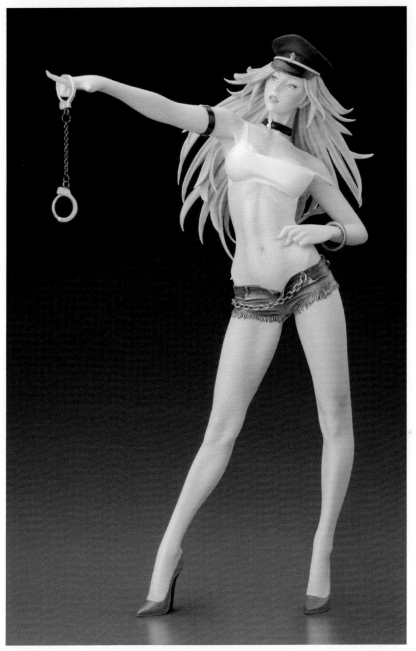

Roxy from the brawler *Final Fight* (Capcom, 1991) is one of the few transgender video game characters.

*Playboy: The Mansion* (Arush, 2005) added nudity to the popular *Sims* genre.

*The Sims 2: Nightlife* (EA, 2005) emphasized relationships over sex, though there was heavy petting.

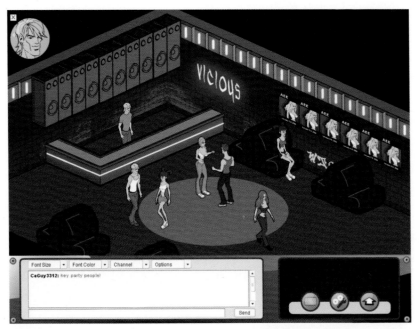

*Naughty America: The Game* (Naughty America, 2005) made a stir at the annual gaming convention, but ultimately was never released.

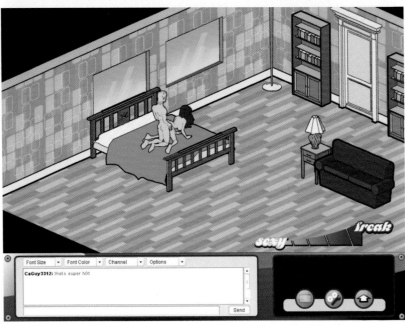

*Naughty America: The Game* (Naughty America, 2005) was the popular adult website's attempt at online virtual sex.

Protagonist Jimmy Hopkins could make out with other prep school boys in *Bully* (Rockstar, 2006).

In the volleyball simulator *Dead or Alive Xtreme Beach Volleyball* (Tecmo, 2006), players could dress their character up in tiny outfits.

Technically a sports title, *Dead or Alive Xtreme Beach Volleyball* (Tecmo, 2006) dedicated hours of gameplay to girl watching.

The popular action game *God of War 2* (Sony, 2007) had interactive sex scenes, as did its predecessor.

*Dead or Alive 4* (Tecmo, 2006) was the first version of the fighting game on the Microsoft XBox 360 next generation system.

Eidos celebrated a decade of Lara Croft with *Tomb Raider: Anniversary Edition* (Eidos, 2007), a revamp of the original hit.

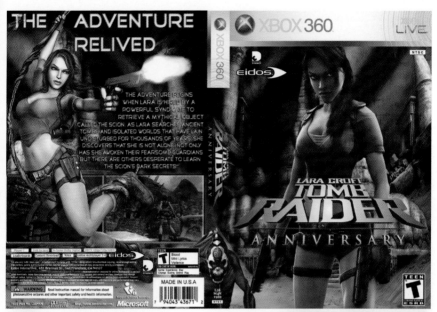

Lara Croft, featured here in *Tomb Raider: Anniversary Edition* (Eidos, 2007), was the first video game sex symbol.

In 2006, Jon M. Gibson and Chris Carle released Nerdcore, the first nude video game calendar. Miss November is playing a classic Nintendo Gameboy.

The first well-known pornographic title in Japan was 1983's *Night Life*, a good year after the notorious *Custer's Revenge* was released in America. Koei, an upstart game publisher, released it for the Fujitsu FM7 home computer. The back cover features two outlined figures in six positions: 69, doggystyle (floor), doggystyle (table), on the knees, missionary and a complex spooning angle. A rhythm method calculator and a sex diary were included. *Night Life* became Koei's first hit. The company followed up with another title, one that loosely translates to "The Tempting Housewife Next Door." Koei pulled out of the virtual sex market early, later making a name for itself with historically accurate Japanese war simulation games. Following Koei's lead with its so-called "romantic education tool," publishers began making erotic games with a traditional spin. Several popular arcade games updated Mahjong, the ancient tile game. A coy virtual vixen will lie in the background as you, her opponent, decide which tiles to remove. Based on your table skill, she will start to disrobe. Adult Mahjong and card-based games fill the average Tokyo arcade, rows of erotic entertainment blended with ancient diversions.

The biggest bridge between classic and modern entertainment, however, would be through a century-old business in rural Japan. In 1889, artist Fusajiro Yamauchi started a small craft company, Nintendo Koppai. He specialized in making playing cards call hanafuda, or "flower cards." Yamauchi-san made a modest living, enough to take care of his family, but his business blossomed when a neighborhood organization took interest in his product. "In the absence of horse or dog racing or sports pools, the *yakuza*, Japan's equivalent of the Mafia, operated high-stakes games of *hanafuda* in casino-like parlors. Nintendo profited handsomely, since professional players would begin each new game with a fresh deck, discarding the old one," David Sheff writes in *Game Over: Nintendo's Battle To Dominate Videogames*.

Nintendo would expand into other forms of entertainment, focusing on electronic goods as computers became more affordable. In Fall 1985 it released the Nintendo Entertainment System, the biggest American game system launch since the Atari 2600 a decade before. The NES included two games, two controllers and two accessories: A red plastic gun called the Zapper and a foot-high midriff-twisting machine called R.O.B. the Robot. The Zapper is a "light gun" that makes the screen flash when you pull the trigger, used to kill fowl in the packed-in game *Duck Hunt*. R.O.B. the Robot turns in a semi-circle and moves a set of spinning tops in conjunction with the action game *Gyromite*. The NES would only be available at toy stores, no computer or electronic stores, and it could not be purchased without also buying the plastic accessories. The 1983 Japanese version was called the Nintendo Family Computer, or Famicom, but it was renamed the Nintendo Entertainment System to disassociate it with technology. Nintendo wanted to show the United States that the NES was a toy, not a game machine, unlike the expensive Ataris and Colecovisions that now grew rusty in American closets. Nintendo's chief game architect, Shigeru Miyamoto, designed *The Legend of Zelda*, *Super Mario Bros.* and other games that took full advantage of the system. The cutting-edge technology allowed better graphics, improved interaction and complex narratives that weren't possible on the decade-old Atari 2600.

Nintendo also brought the Nintendo Seal of Quality. Comparable to a Good Housekeeping approval, a golden Seal of Quality on the box was to insure customers that Nintendo knew the content of the respective video game and decided it was appropriate to play. According to author Brenda Brathwaite, former Nintendo of America senior vice president Howard Lincoln listed the company's standards as follows:

**No sexually suggestive or explicit content**
**No sexist language or depictions**
**No random, gratuitous, or excessive violence**
**No graphic illustration of death**
**No domestic violence or abuse**
**No excessive force in sports games**
**No ethnic, racial or religious, or sexual stereotypes**
**No profanity or obscenity**
**No use of drugs, smoking material, or alcohol**
**No subliminal political messages or overt political statements**

Lincoln elaborated, "Among the sexual content Nintendo deemed inappropriate were women dressed as Playboy Bunnies, men whistling at women, a woman who 'shakes her breasts,' and a game in which a female's clothing did not 'adequately cover her body.'" Nintendo's restrictions did not seem much different than the Comic Book Code of 1954, which required that women "… be drawn realistically without exaggeration of any physical qualities" and that "Illicit sex relations are neither to be hinted at or portrayed," or even Hollywood's earlier Hays Code of 1930, which carried a whole section on depicting "impure love." According to the Hays Code, impure love means intimacy outside of marriage, "… love which society has always regarded as wrong and which has been banned by divine law." However, if filmmakers feel they have to show impure love, "It must not be presented in such a way to arouse passion or morbid curiosity on the part of the audience."

By Holiday 1987 the Nintendo Entertainment System was the number one selling toy, surpassing Cabbage Patch Kids and Teddy Ruxpin. Other companies also prospered. *Voltron, Robotech* and similar cartoons captured adolescent imaginations by combining high-tech machines, soap opera subplots and quirky Japanese humor. In 1988, Katsuhiro Otomo brought *Akira* to America. The animated movie was about three gang member teenagers fighting a monster made out of "pure energy," trying to put Tokyo under nuclear attack. There is a rape scene, limbs are severed and adolescent bodies are squished like cow eyes under a hammer. It became required watching for any boy under 16, and culturists well beyond puberty loved it, too—even critic Roger Ebert gave it a thumbs up. *Akira* was recognized both critically and commercially because it was a perfect example of what Japan does best: take pop art seriously.

Japan also exerted its heavy influence in 1980s American commerce, a turnabout from decades as the economic underdog. In 1973 the Organization of Petroleum Exporting Countries, or OPEC, inflated gas prices for profit. The oil crisis made cash-tight Americans more dependent on the small, fuel efficient Japanese cars. A second OPEC price jump, in 1979, doubled United States gas prices. Honda and Nissan established plants in Ohio and Tennessee, respectively. The Japanese auto industry ended up dominating Henry Ford's America in both sales and productivity. Unused to creating cars with a Japanese level of efficiency, GM, Chrysler and Ford were losing money, closing plants or selling them to Japanese companies. Only 40 years before, the World War II Allies, led by America and Britain, had decimated much of the Asian country's infrastructure. "In 1947, the year of the transistor's invention, American aid to Japan exceeded $400 million. To help pull Japanese industry back onto its feet, the U.S. would provide technological assistance and encourage Japan to undertake research and development," according to Bob Johnstone's *We Were Burning: Japanese Entrepreneurs and the Forging of the Electronic Age*. Hewlett Packard, Texas Instruments and other American companies created the transistor, compact disc laser technology and high-resolution television. Nearly all the technical research was licensed, if not outright given to the Japanese. Johnstone cites various political and economic reasons for this. "There was, however, still another reason why U.S. concerns were prepared to transfer their technology to Japan so blithely: Simply, in their wildest dreams, the Americans never imagined that the Japanese would catch up to them so quickly."

■ ■ ■

Started by cocksure American entrepreneur Nolan Bushnell, Atari had managed to exile its founder and lose billions during the 1983 video game crash. It was now looking for an Atari 2600 follow-up to fight Nintendo. The company released the Atari 5200 and the Atari 7800, two systems that were technically inferior to the NES. Neither sold well. At the arcades, Japanese company Capcom released *Final Fight*, a mindless, yet addictive combat game that established the side-scrolling fighting genre which would dominate arcades the next five years. Atari would respond with *Pit Fighter*, a stiff battle arcade game composed of stilted digital pictures reminiscent of Jean-Claude Van Damme movies. Capcom again replied with *Street Fighter II: The World Warrior*, which became the most imitated one-on-one fighting game in arcade history. Unlike the seventies, Atari didn't have hit arcade games to draw customers to its home systems and third-party companies like Capcom and Konami decided to bring their games to Nintendo instead. Atari lost a foothold both at home and the arcade, and there was no other American company qualified to take the lead.

The newly profitable home and arcade market encouraged other Japanese companies to reenter the American video game industry. One publisher, Kaneko, released three arcade games within one year: the *Final Fight*-inspired *DJ Boy*, the frantic shooter *Aero Blasters* and the puzzle title *Gal's Panic*. *Gal's Panic* is a revamp of Taito's *Qix*, a 1981 arcade hit released around the time Kaneko was last relevant. In *Qix*, you drop a continuous line that, when made into a box, paints the enclosed area. The goal is to paint 75 percent of the screen while avoiding two enemies: a spinning electric wand and a set of sparks walking along the box borders. You are only vulnerable to the wand's attacks when out painting, but are exposed to the sparks when sitting on the wall. You have to keep moving. *Qix's* basic graphics and electronic, florescent backgrounds made the game more *Tron* than *Ms. Pac-Man*, giving it a nerdy glow. Arcade games have an Attract Mode, a demo that repeats when people aren't playing. The Attract Mode for *Gal's Panic* begins with purple, red and orange bubbles rising to the top of the screen and popping to spell out G-A-L-S P-A-N-I-C in irregular letters. A spinning pink bow flies under the game's title and a chipper Japanese woman says "Good luck!," calling passersby to deposit a coin.

Once the game starts, the first thing you see is "GAL SELECT" in big rainbow letters above six Japanese profiles. They are relatively chubby, round faces, and seem to still be working off puberty. There is smiling Marina, in a stylish haircut and bedazzled earrings, dour Emi, with a serious face packing a strained smile, and four other women. The game has three rounds. In the first area, a fast-moving spider spits tiny arachnids and webs to slow you down. The second area has a very fast moving fireball shooting little killer flames. The final area has a ridiculously fast moving pyramid capable of splitting itself into a dozen separate pieces, all bouncing off into different directions. In the background, underneath the chaos, is a cartoon silhouette of the woman you selected. She is fully clothed during the first round, in her underwear during the second and completely nude in the final round. Successfully creating boxes over the body reveals her skin. Making boxes over her body also requires energy, which is tracked by an onscreen meter. Hit a certain low point and the curvy silhouette will turn into a random picture which could be, among other things, a blue female bear wearing red lipstick or a bloody figure that resembles the pinhead character from *Hellraiser*. To win the round and see the woman, you have to make boxes in the area around her silhouette, which adds energy, until the meter is long enough to complete the act. The women give encouragement, "You and I are going to have fun!" and "Good!" Unbox the vagina, breast or belly button in the final round and you receive more colorful commentary. "Ohhhh, good," Ayami might say in a muffled voice, as if she's speaking with her face in a soft pillow. If you manage to uncover 80 percent of her body, a visual round of claps appears and a long note of striptease music plays. The cartoon representation of the woman is star wiped away and replaced with a photo of the real model. She is usually kneeling or bending down to the floor. She looks younger than the cartoon drawing. The model squeaks once last thing, "Touch my body" or perhaps "Hold me!," and the game returns to the GAL SELECT menu.

*Gal's Panic* was an American sleeper hit in 1990, but in Japan it fit well with the erotic Mahjong and card games genre. Kaneko made at least six sequels. In America none were as popular as the original, which is enough of a moneymaker that it can still be found in modern American arcades – albeit in a dark corner. "Regular *Qix* wills the player into doing things within the context of the game. You want to create tiny boxes, but for some reason you think 'Oh my God, I can do a huge box and I can get all this area!' and, of course, you get hit by the enemy and die," said *Power Up* author Kohler. "For *Gal's Panic*, it's even more intense because of what's under there. It is all the more reason for the player to act like a total idiot, waste his 100 yen and play it again."

Another notable sexual arcade game in Japan would be from Taff Systems, a Korean company. On *Boong-Ga Boong-Ga*, the unit's top half has the usual TV screen, but the bottom has a bottom: a person's behind and legs, slightly bent as if picking something up. He or she is wearing tight jeans. The mannequin makes it look like someone is halfway inside the arcade machine, perhaps trying to repair a loose nut. Next to the butt is a large, removable plastic finger. *Boong-Ga Boong-Ga* translates into "Spank 'em" in English, but the game is actually an anal penetration simulator, hence the plastic finger (as opposed to a hand) and the drawings of whipped, multicolored flying poo on its marquee. "This is a fun game of spanking peopple [sic] that make your life miserable," said the arcade flyer. "When you spank the character that you choose to punish, the face [sic] expression of the character will change as they scream and twitch in pain. The funny face [sic] expressions will make people laugh and relieve the stress." It lists eight characters you can make scream and twitch in pain: "an ex-girlfriend, an ex-boyfriend, a gangster, the mother-in-law, a gold digger, a prostitute, a child molester and a con artist." "…the game was received enthusiastically [in Tokyo] last year," wrote *WIRED*. "Taff System recently signed a deal to distribute 200 Boong-Ga Boong-Ga machines in arcades all across Japan."

THE PORN ERA: OTAKU

■ ■ ■

Tomonobu Itagaki is a tall, pale man, probably in his forties, with shiny black hair down to his shoulders, dark clothing and pale, acne-scared skin. Perpetually sunglassed, most gamers have never seen his eyes. He could be a Japanese member of The Ramones. Itagaki-san has worked for only one company, Tecmo, a medium-sized game publisher in Tokyo. He went there straight from college after deciding against becoming a professional Mahjong player. His first assignment was *Super Tecmo Bowl*, Tecmo's popular sports franchise. "I guess I can take credit for having snow in the game," he said in an interview. "In fact, that's the only thing I did for that game." (*Super Tecmo Bowl* was one of the first sports games to incorporate weather.) Itagaki-san decided that for his next project he would try designing a complex 3D fighting game. He called it *Dead or Alive*, not for the game's deadly martial arts, but because Tecmo was in financial trouble: it needed a hit or it was going under. (Game designer Hironobu Sakaguchi named Square's legendary adventure series *Final Fantasy* for the same reason.)

*Dead or Alive* was a hit. The 1996 brawler had colorful 3D environments and visuals that pushed the respective platforms – the Sony PlayStation and the Sega Saturn – to previously unknown heights. It also did well in arcades worldwide. Classic one-on-one fighting games like Data East's *Karate Champ* and Konami's *Yie Ar Kung Fu* were popular in the early eighties, but Itagaki-san's title joined an arcade resurgence led by Capcom's *Street Fighter*, Sega's *Virtua Fighter*, Midway's *Mortal Kombat* and Namco's *Tekken*. By the time *Dead or Alive 2* arrived in 1999, Itagaki-san openly gave his opinion of the competition: *Tekken* wasn't that good and, frankly, *Mortal Kombat* was of low quality. He had little to nothing good to say about the remaining fighting games. From *Tekken*'s blocking system to *Virtua Fighter*'s innovations in three dimensions, *Dead or Alive* would probably not have been as progressive of a fighting game without its predecessors – something the designer was loathe to admit. It was as if *Dead or Alive* played Athena to the competition's Zeus, appearing fully formed without anyone else's intervention.

Tecmo's follow-up *Dead or Alive 2* wasn't as much of a leap in gameplay as it was a study in detail. Spinning leaves fall from the semi-nude trees onto the battlefield below. A well-timed kick knocks a character through a dojo wall, exposing the outer perimeter of the arena. The sun glistens off in the distance, creating a bit of lens flare. The female characters, of which there are many, shake spherical, buoyant breasts, tugged by some unknown centrifugal force as they walk, run, kick and jump. *Dead or Alive 2* sold significantly better than its predecessor, and Itagaki-san began developing *DOA 2* "remixes" on different platforms. He did several redesigns of another Tecmo franchise, *Ninja Gaiden*, by adjusting the difficulty, improving the graphics and re-releasing it on the newest gaming hardware. For *Dead or Alive*, he kept tweaking the breast physics. They had to be perfect. "*DOA* is known for its bouncing breasts," he would later say, citing the little-known 2D fighting game *Garou Densetsu* as the first game he saw with a considerable "jiggle factor." "Of course, when I applied it to a 3D game, it was almost too much for people."

Popularity increased with *Dead or Alive 3* and the *DOA* spinoff *Dead or Alive Xtreme Volleyball*. In the sports game Zack, a fighter from *Dead or Alive*, purchases a deserted island, builds a casino and tricks all the *DOA* characters (at least all the female ones) to come there for a free vacation. Previously ruthless adversaries, the trapped ladies begin playing games together, rubbing each other's backs and generally getting to know each other better. As the omnipotent voyeur, you tell the women where to go, what to wear and where to touch. There is an occasional volleyball match to earn extra points, which in turn can be spent on buying more outfits for the women. Despite the game's title, it's easier to find the women in a jumping race across floating wafers or a butt-bumping balance battle on a log. They are almost always bouncing and are almost always wet. *Dead or Alive Xtreme Volleyball* received a M for Mature rating from the Electronic Software Ratings Board, roughly the equivalent of a movie R, and reviewers panned the title. "Watching boobs bouncing about independent of one another made me seasick," said one reviewer. It spent months on the American top ten sales charts, and Itagaki-san churned out a sequel, *Dead or Alive Xtreme Volleyball 2*, with similar results. He would turn out more *Dead or Alive* remixes in upcoming years. (He would also be sued by a female coworker for allegedly groping and forcibly French-kissing her during a shared afterwork cab ride.)

In Japan, Tecmo began selling dozens, if not hundreds of different *Dead or Alive* porcelain figures. One character, a young, buxom brunette, wears a slim black bikini and leans back, playfully, spread eagle on a water raft from *Dead or Alive Xtreme Volleyball*. The popular Japanese importer J-List sold it for $83. In one post, the videogame website *Kotaku* listed the newest Japanese *Dead or Alive* products including a real woman's bikini emblazoned with the characters, a bendable doll and a life-sized "body pillow" of a lead character. The final item shown was a mouse pad with two raised lumps. "In case you're not sure how to use the mousepad, the folks at ChestRest, who make them, have included some basic Dos and Don'ts: Do place your wrist between Kasumi's well-endowed breasts; Don't hug and then fall in love with Kasumi's breasts; DON'T even think about placing her breasts against your crotch and then pumping your arm in the air while shouting: Woo! Woo! Woo!" *Kotaku* titled the post "Play with Kasumi's Breasts for $25." It later noted, "Just because *Dead or Alive Xtreme 2* didn't exactly set the world on fire, doesn't mean its game goods can't. (And some will argue that the series is now produced to sell certain segments of the population life-sized character pillows.)"

 *Dead or Alive Xtreme Volleyball* fits into a Japanese game genre called bishoujo, or "pretty girl." The goal is to pleasure or have fun with the women in the game. (The genre can also be called *hentai*.) Megatech's 1992 PC adventure *Cobra Mission* was the first major bishoujo title to come to America. You play JR Knight, a detective searching for missing women in the shadier parts of Florida. It has a top-down view, not unlike *Pac-Man*, and the characters, including your handsome gumshoe, are short and stocky. Successfully follow the clues to a damsel in distress and *Cobra Mission* shifts to a detailed, first-person view close-up of the woman. A list of options appears. You are given a limited amount of turns to pleasure her. A traditional set of choices:

**Use your hand**
**Use your lips**
**Whisper**
**Rotary Vibrator**
**Vibrator**
**Candle**
**READY to GO!!**

Megatech released a "R" version with limited nudity, but players could purchase or later upgrade to an "X" version with more graphic visuals. The box reads, "Cobra Mission (TM) graphics are drawn by established Anime artists in Japan. Our Anime girls are wonderfully fresh and unique – sporting flashy eyes, fine noses and spunky hair colors. You'll be dazzled by 190+ high-resolution Anime graphics including 50 solely for the sexier moments of play." The text is bracketed by four photos, including a group shot that looks like it may be the prelude to a large orgy. "So provocative is Cobra Mission (TM) you'll find yourself reacting both physically and emotionally!!!"

Japan also had a parallel genre equally popular to bishoujo. In Masuya's PlayStation 2 game *Choaniki: Legend of Holy Protein*, two well-greased bodybuilders, Adon and Samson, fly through space shooting evil aliens. They are ripped, evenly tanned and don heavily-weighed thongs. A video game poster shows the pair facing each other, holding hands, smiling, in a standing action pose, leaning on their toes forward as if the next frame would show them wrestling. One character has his knee securely between the other's thighs. Originally for the Japanese PC Engine system, *Choaniki* was a descendent of Konami's eighties spaceship title *Gradius*. While the classic bad guys were multitentacled extraterrestrials and wide battleships, *Choaniki: Legend of Holy Protein* had half-naked human-looking beings. The heroes fend them off by shooting sparkly white blasts from the tops of their heads. They are after the holy protein, a powerful substance that will give them the perfect bodies. (Protein is also a major component of human sperm.) A similar title, D3 Publishing's *The Friendship Adventure* for the PlayStation 2, casts you as a young new broadcaster who must bond with other males on staff both in the office and after work. The locations vary from beer-soaked sports bars to sweaty saunas. The goal is to get as close as possible to your desired mentor. "One of the more revolutionary details put into the game is after you input your name, you can set if you're the 'giver' or 'receiver' *(ahem)*," noted the website *GayGamer.net*. "You can also set any of the NPC's sexuality as 'Gay' or 'Non-gay.' The characters end up [having orgasms] either way, but the dialogue and story flow changes depending on your choice." It adds, "The original PC adaptation is recognized as one of the first games that was made specifically for the gay market in Japan." Japanese games exploring yaoi, which literally translates to "boy love," usually aren't geared towards gay men, but to young women. According to *Power Up*, "...

[T]here are dating games that put the female player into the role of a male high school student who goes after other male high school students. One… is called *Gakuen Heaven: Boys' Love Scramble*. Its box proclaims it a 'Love Love Hyper Boys Game.'" Kohler estimates about half of all Japanese computer games sold are pornographic. Peter Payne, owner of the popular import site J-List, explains how in the book *Sex in Video Games*. "Since, over the years, some of the bishoujo game titles released in Japan have caused concern about their negative influences on society, the industry is currently self-regulated, through an organization called the Software Morality Association (Sof-Rin) which sets standards for the games. No characters under 18, no themes such as incest or bestiality, and so on. For the most part, these efforts keep the bishoujo game industry out of trouble as far as the law is concerned. Part of the reason why adult dating-sims get extra leeway is that they aren't live-action and aren't really viewed as porn in a real sense." American arms of publishers like Nintendo and Sony are much more conservative than their counterparts, so most bishoujo-style games would have to be purchased through import companies like J-List. *Choaniki*, *The Friendship Adventure* and *Gakuen Heaven: Boys' Love Scramble* never made it to the United States.

Sega's PlayStation 2 title *Rez* was one of the few provocative Japanese games to make it to America. A fast-paced shooter, you play a programmer who enters a hostile computer world. It used vector graphics, visuals composed solely of straight lines, to convey the sparse universe. The background music adjusts to your actions so you, in a sense, are creating a rhythm as you play. *Rez* came with a mouse-inspired peripheral, about five inches long and three inches wide, which shook to the rhythm. It was called the Trance Vibrator. "You can put in anywhere – your foot, your back, your waist," *Rez* designer Tetsuya Mizuguchi told *Wired*. "It's up to our customers' imagination." It also came with a "washable protective pouch." Sony gave the game an "E for Everyone" rating.

Sega never admitted it, but *Rez* utilized teledildonics, a new field where heavy-automated vibrators and other machines are used in a directly sexual manner. Similarly inspired, Kyle Machulis of the sex and tech website Slashdong created a vibrating dildo and butt plug that connected directly to the Microsoft XBox system. It would be called the SexBox. However, Sega's *Rez* was the first major video game to feature teledildonics. The PlayStation

2 version proved to be the most popular, but *Rez* was originally released on the Dreamcast, Sega's own late nineties system that failed in the American marketplace. Overseas, the Sega Dreamcast maintained a solid Japanese user base based on a continual stream of bootleg pornographic games. Erotica publishers *would* eventually stop producing for the Dreamcast – about six years after Sega stopped manufacturing the system.

# THE LARA CROFT ERA
## (1996 – 2001)

From a pure design standpoint, Lara Croft herself actually isn't that amazing – she's the equivalent of a stick figure with huge boobs. Still, her name does serve as excellent shorthand for a sea change, like when you say "Eminem" or "George W. Bush": There is an immediate thought, a rush to opinion, a "for" or "against" and, most importantly, a before and an after. In Lara's "after," well-adjusted men were contemplating fucking a bunch of pixels, lusting after a digital diva that didn't exist – and actually admitting it to other people! It's no coincidence she blossomed at the dawn of mainstream Internet porn (though, with online pictures and video, you at least know that person is out there… somewhere). Lara represents the first time America fell in lust with the *idea* of someone in a video game, as much as a comic reader may have for Jean Grey in The Dark Phoenix Saga, or as I did with the liberated Madame Bovary in Gustave Flaubert's classic novel. Video games now had the power to ignite sexual passion.

However, those passions were still diffused through other pop cultural identities, and the three major characters of this era – Lara Croft, the virtual Sims, the lesbians of *Fear Effect 2: Retro Helix* – are still caricatures of norms established by Pamela Anderson, Reality TV and the movie *Bound*, in that order. They managed to make people horny, but video games still weren't their own cultural force.

# VIRGINS

On Independence Day 1997, a probe landed on the red planet. Called the Mars Pathfinder, the small NASA-created vehicle carried an even smaller land rover named Sojourner. The rover was a photojournalist. Sojourner would crawl over the red desert surface, trolling for interesting items and taking pictures at NASA's request. The rover would explore areas that, at -220 degrees Fahrenheit, would break the human body apart like shattered ice.

Over the following four months it would show us what had never been seen by the human eye. Nightly news would end with the latest widescreen Mars photo. Scientists pontificated about possible extra-terrestrial life. The media took a renewed interest in H.G. Wells, Jules Verne and other future-oriented authors. Using a new medium called the Internet, NASA would post photographs on its website shortly after they were taken. Users could select the Mars pictures they liked best and download as many photos as their 28.8k baud modems could handle.

During Neil Armstrong's 1969 moon landing, the Americans in New York and the Americans in California looking at their television sets were watching the exact same footage at the exact same time. It was a shared experience. It was also a generic experience. During the Mars probe thirty years later, viewers could go online at, say, three in the morning to see if there were any new photos. Passionate fans could enter forums or chat rooms and argue about the existence of extra terrestrials. They could set their favorite Mars photo as a computer desktop picture. Utilizing the World Wide Web, NASA allowed each viewer to create his or her own unique connection to Mars. By its final transmission on September 27, 1997, the Mars Pathfinder and Sojourner sent more than 16,000 pictures of the red planet's surface. Technology was extending the arm of human experiences. It just happened to be a robot arm. As groundbreaking as the Mars mission may have been,

Americans didn't necessarily learn the true power of the Internet by looking at porous crimson rocks and dried river valleys. They learned earlier that summer, at their workplace office, in their dens, in front of their televisions, as they watched clips of Pamela Anderson fucking her husband, Tommy. Internet discussions and media coverage related to *Pam & Tommy Lee: Hardcore & Uncensored* trumped the historical Mars visit. Porn pundits argue that it was downloaded or bought online several times over any Mars-related paraphernalia. In retrospect, it seems that Pamela Anderson Lee was the real uncharted world.

The twenty nine year old bleach blonde was a worldwide star thanks to *Baywatch*, a popular lifeguard show that featured a good-looking cast of men and women saving good-looking bad swimmers. The title sequence slowed down as Lee ran down the beach, her 36DD breasts restlessly bounding in her tight red suit. A poster of her in the *Baywatch* swimsuit was a bestseller, a staple for adolescent rooms and college dorms. Her husband, Tommy Lee, had just reunited with his group, Motley Crue. Known for hits "Dr. Feelgood" and "Girls Girls Girls," the once-popular eighties rock band had gone out of favor, gotten into drugs and fallen out with each other. The drummer wanted the band to make a comeback and hoped that the ongoing recording sessions for the next album, *Generation Swine*, would provide one. It was during this hectic time that the newlyweds took their houseboat to Lake Mead, Nevada, for a five-day vacation. They decided to take a video camera.

Tommy Lee claims that the grainy, seventy-six minute tape was stolen from his family vault by a disgruntled personal assistant. The tape ended up in the hands of Seth Warshavsky, a twenty-three year old Internet mogul and owner of the Internet Entertainment Group. He contacted Tommy Lee and told him he was going to broadcast the tape on the Internet. The couple sued IEG, but the courts ruled that, since they were public figures, the content was newsworthy and Warshavsky could show the footage. He would eventually release it on VHS, but for now it would be streamed – shown "live" – from the IEG members-only website ClubLove. Warshavsky said millions joined ClubLove to watch the sex video, and millions of dollars were definitely made from the notorious video tape. Pamela and Tommy Lee would eventually be awarded $1.5 million in damages, as well as attorney fees, but no amount of money could take the video out of

America's hands. Years later Tommy Lee was still livid. "It pissed me off – because I don't ever want my kids to go to a friend's house and find a video in the VCR of their parents fucking."

Pamela Anderson began modeling for beer companies in the mid-eighties. She quickly got a *Playboy* centerfold, followed by a stint as the tool girl on the hit ABC show *Home Improvement*. In 1992 she joined *Baywatch*, making her tight breast-implant filled red swimsuit an icon in itself. In *Barb Wire*, a 1996 movie based on a comic, she wore a tight one-piece leather catsuit for the role, the top turning into a low-cut bustier that pushed up her breasts together. The movie bombed at the box office, dashing her goals of transitioning from televisions to theaters. *Barb Wire* was nominated for a Razzie Award Worst Picture, but lost to the $50 million Demi Moore movie *Striptease*. (Moore's movie also won Razzie's Worst Actress, Worst Director, Worst Original Song, Worst Screen Couple and Worst Screenplay.) The film followed a single mom stripper and her coworkers, but *Striptease* also featured Demi Moore's new breasts. They were big, buoyant and spherical, and made her look less like the girl next door seen in *Ghost*.

Aside from silicon, both *Striptease* and *Barb Wire* shared another element. *Striptease* shows a stripper who never takes it all off for the movie audience. *Barb Wire* features a ruthless sexy action hero who never copulates. Neither hormonally-aggressive character is ever nude. On Times Square, Calvin Klein crafted multistory billboards featuring an underwear-clad Mark Wahlberg. In Congress, conservatives and liberals argued over if sex education classes promoted sexuality and whether condoms should be distributed in the school. It seemed okay to sell sex appeal and to imply sexual situations, but not to actually have it. With *Pam & Tommy Lee: Hardcore & Uncensored*, the famous *Baywatch* actress had crossed the line. She publicly gave up the goods. The virgin/whore archetype was ruined. There was nothing more to see.

Pamela Anderson Lee would be replaced on *Baywatch* the following year.

■ ■ ■

There are several myths in the video game industry. In one, a young, geeky game designer named Toby Gard was working on a new character, one he would later describe as a female Indiana Jones. She was originally Larry Croft, but he thought a female character would be more appealing. It would be a 3D game, not one that would require glasses, but one that would have physical depth. You would feel like the character was going into the screen. Each item onscreen would be made up of polygons, geometric shapes that could be manipulated to scale and, therefore, make 3D levels easier. As you got closer to an object, the polygon scale would increase and it becomes bigger, and the opposite as you walk away. The characters themselves would also be composed of polygons and the game artists would use special graphic software to create them. So far, this is all true. The myth is that Gard was in the offices of Core Design, the UK-based development company, working on his new female heroine when, on a whim, he made her breast size 150 percent bigger than normal. Officemates noticed and encouraged him to keep the design… at least for a little while. Gard went along with the joke. This well-told story of how Lara Croft received 38 DD breasts seems much more likely when you realize that Toby Gard was only nineteen years old.

Ms. Pac Man was perhaps the first video game heroine, but she was not created by the game manufacturer, Bally. In 1981, nine MIT students reprogrammed the *Pac-Man* machines they leased to local stores. They modified the mazes and made the frantic game even faster. The crew then went a step further, creating a special circuit board that, when added to a normal *Pac-Man* machine, automatically upgraded it to their special version. Now they could sell the board to arcade owners who didn't want to risk breaking their expensive units. The students first tried it with another popular game, Atari's *Missile Command*. As they completed the work on *Pac-Man*, Atari caught wind of the *Missile Command* board and sued them before they could sell any. The game company then did something unprecedented: Atari offered the kids a contract to make Atari games provided they, of course, stop manufacturing modification boards. They agreed. Contract in hand, the MIT students went straight to Bally, showed them the modified *Pac-Man* board and started negotiating. Coincidently, Bally had no idea how to follow up the most popular video game ever made. It asked them to modify their enhancement board to create an official *Pac-Man* sequel. Their first decision was to make the new Pac-Man a woman, later adding a red bow tie and a beauty mark. (The game would also have intermissions with Pac Man and Ms. Pac Man chasing each other, locking lips and eventually having a baby Pac Man, making it arguably the first sex scene in a mainstream video game.) The next notable heroine was Samus Aran, the tough bounty hunting space warrior in Nintendo's *Metroid*. (The game seemed inspired by Sigourney Weaver's *Alien* movies, the second of which came out in 1986, the same year as *Metroid*.) The twist was that the gamer wasn't told her gender. You spend hours playing through the lengthy adventure, starting at and guiding the innocuous figure in a full body metal space suit. It wasn't until the end, as the credits were about to roll, that the warrior would stare at the screen, towards you, and emerge out of the shapeless protective covering to reveal a purple dancer's leotard and long, very green hair. Well before email or the Internet became commonplace, Samus Aran's true identity remained a secret that was slowly exposed to skilled individuals who beat the game. Those who completed *Metroid* under the time limit could play Samus's adventure again – without the body armor. *Metroid* aside, most female characters were accents to the main male characters, like the Valkrie in the popular 1985 dungeon crawler *Gauntlet*, who, among three other warriors, was the token woman, or Chun Li, the single female in 1992's seminal *Street Fighter II: The World Warrior*. Valkrie wore a revealing metal bustier, similar in shape to the *Barb Wire* outfit, and was later upgraded to a furry two-piece bikini worthy of Raquel Welch in *One Million Years B.C.*. Chun Li initially wore a blue Asian top, Princess Leia-style earmuffs and a tiny skirt. Skilled gamers could time her kicks just right to see her cotton white panties. These were female characters before Lara Croft.

Gard and the Core Design team spent eighteen months creating *Tomb Raider featuring Lara Croft*, a game best described as an intelligent shooter. Unlike *Doom* and other combat-focused precursors, *Tomb Raider* split gameplay evenly between perilous shootouts and brain-teasing puzzles. Lara also had the option of holstering her guns – a first in modern video games – which allowed her to scale cliffs, grab swinging vines and, perhaps, even think before reacting. A smart woman, the character would be the daughter of Lord Henshingly Croft. She would speak in proper English with a proper British accent. She would live in a manor. "…[S]he was supposed to be this strong woman, this upper-class adventurer," Gard said. He also acknowledged some not-so-obvious source material. "Lara was based on elements of Indiana Jones, Tank Girl, and, people always say, my sister," Gard later told a British newspaper. "Maybe subconsciously she was my sister."

Core Design was a development company, not a publisher, but it connected with another small British outfit named Eidos Interactive to distribute *Tomb Raider*. The development company is the artist, the publisher the proverbial salesman. The publisher will often fund the development company's projects and ideally facilitate the peace and quiet it needs to create. It will also work on brand recognition, organizing media junkets and other forms of public relations. When royalties arrive, it is the one that cuts the check.

It is heavily rumored that Eidos faced bankruptcy before its deal with Core Design. *Tomb Raider* could have literally been a make-or-break title, which turned the Eidos PR machine into overdrive. The company released promotional pictures of the buxom character in tight bathing suits and clingy cocktail dresses. *Maxim* and other men's magazines published her pictures and her dimensions: 38-24-34. Gucci paid Eidos $30,000 for Lara to pose in the famous house's latest couture. (It used virtual clothing.) English nude model Neil McAndrew was hired to play Lara Croft at marketing events. Gard, an employee on the company payroll, had nothing to do with Lara's presentation to the public. "She wasn't [meant to be] a tits-out-for-the-lads type of character in any way. Quite the opposite, in fact. I thought that what was interesting about her was she was this unattainable, austere, dangerous sort of person," he said in an interview. Eidos took the untouchable character out of Gard's hands and made you feel like she was in yours. Gard's ice queen became public domain. Angry and disillusioned, Gard quit Core Design two months after the game's release. He started a new development studio, Confounding Factor, and a new project, a pirate game named *Galleon*. "*Galleon* is not a progression from *Tomb Raider*," he declared. "It is simply what *Tomb Raider* should have been." His new found venture wouldn't be burning up much *Tomb Raider* money. By leaving Core, Toby lost his share of the estimated $700 million.

■ ■ ■

On November 15, 1996, *Tomb Raider* was released for the Sega Saturn, the PC and, soon thereafter, the new Sony PlayStation. *Tomb Raider* sold three million copies within the first year, and was a critical and commercial success. By November 1997 Eidos shot out a sequel, *Tomb Raider II*, and *Tomb Raider III: Adventures of Lara Croft* arrived the November after that. The next *Tomb Raider, The Last Revelation*, would again be out the following November, to which one critic said, "This latest Tomb Raider can be rewarding for those who can suffer through its cumbersome controls, numerous high difficult gameplay sequences, and occasional bugs." *Tomb Raider* sales remained relatively high, but the numbers for each successive game dropped significantly. Critics said Eidos and Core Design did little to improve the games, and it certainly didn't help that *Tomb Raider's* principal designer, Toby Gard, had left the company likely before the first sequel was even outlined. Meanwhile, Lara Croft appeared in original comics and as plastic action figures. U2 commissioned original Lara Croft animations for its sold-out PopArt tour. The band would show the footage on multistory monitors as they performed. She became the 1997 cover girl for the popular British magazine *The Face*. In 1999, Playboy's August cover read "Tomb Raider Nell McAndrew A.K.A. Lara Croft Nude" alongside the then former *Tomb Raider* model posing in an army fatigue-colored bikini. Inside was McAndrew's eight-page nude pictorial alongside digital photographs of Lara. The first has Lara, with a low-cut tank-top and exposed midriff, holding a copy of *Tomb Raider III: Adventures of Lara Croft*. The last has Lara laying down in a small silver bikini, letting her arm with the gun rest on her thigh, right below McAndrew's nude spread.

The Internet flooded with recommended in-game locations, specific areas where, if Lara was turned just right, you could catch a better glimpse of her cleavage. Shortly after the original *Tomb Raider* a small downloadable program called "Nude Raider" appeared on pornographic and gaming websites. The program would superimpose a graphic layer, called a "skin," onto the in-game character. The imaginative skin stripped Lara of all her clothes so gamers could run around the Venetian catacombs nude or skinny dip in digital Peruvian falls. Amateur artists began to make unauthorized digital pictures of Lara. Supported by new, cheaper 3D software and a grateful audience, they would reenact scenes from the game or create new scenarios entirely. "A small number of websites run by fans of the Tomb Raider game series and its heroine Lara Croft post fan-made art that they call 'Nude Raiders,' which show the lovely heroine wither clothes off," the game website *IGN* reported. "Some of the images are even more risqué, showing her bound, cuffed and in other pornographic poses." One memorable digital poster shows Lara sitting on the floor next to her bed. She is topless and only wearing her jeans, knees to her chest to cover her breasts and hands wrapped around her legs. With her pensive look to the door, it looks as if she just got a spanking. By the 1998 release of *Tomb Raider III*, there were hundreds of pieces of Nude Raider art available for free online. Creating one digital image would take dozens, if not hundreds of hours. These posters could be considered the first homage to a digital sex symbol. Keenly focused on ownership and control, Eidos and Core Design sent cease-and-desist letters to the few, but persistent websites dedicated to Nude Raider art. It proved ineffective. In August 1998, Core Design sued an American web host company for $1.1 million to get the rights to *www.nuderaider.com*, home of the supposed ringleader in Lara Croft nude art. "Core bases its action on the argument that it owns the copyright on all forms and permutations of the Lara Croft image," one legal website reported. It won the case and quickly shut down *www.nuderaider.com*, but by then illegal Lara Croft posters had already spread across the Internet faster than a virus. The company would have to search the then billion-or-so World Wide Web pages to find pictures, often renamed or hidden away in unreachable partitions, not to mention the posters that left the Internet and were saved on fans' home computers. Most Nude Raider art was comfortably sitting on people's hard drives next to the illegal Pamela and Tommy Lee sex movie.

Three *Tomb Raider* iterations came and went before Toby Gard finally released his pirate adventure, *Galleon*. It was most often described as an ambitious, yet underwhelming experience. It failed at retail. Gard would come back to the *Tomb Raider* franchise after its fifth game, *Tomb Raider: Angel of Darkness*, was a critical and commercial flop. He would be returning to a new company: Eidos fired Core Design (keeping ownership of *Tomb Raider*) and hired Crystal Dynamics, a small but well-known company behind solid adventure games like *Soul Reaver*. By the time the *Angel of Darkness* follow-up *Tomb Raider: Legend* was released, Lara had changed hands from Toby Gard to Core Design to Eidos to Crystal Dynamics with Toby Gard. Considered a wonderful return to its essence, *Legend* was a huge success on all levels, selling record numbers and getting rave reviews. It didn't seem to change Gard. He would refuse media interviews, even at Eidos's urging, and avoid the limelight as if he was a paparazzi-fazed pop icon himself. The average person may be angry about the millions of dollars lost or creating what critics consider an artistic failure and doing a proverbial return to the nest. For Gard, it seemed to all come back to Lara. An early advertisement spread for *Tomb Raider: Legend* shows Lara's perfect apple bottom in tight khaki shorts and her rock-solid legs standing on a cliff. Off in the distance you can see a grassy valley off cliffside, and beyond that a deep, damp canal, noticeable if you look between her legs. In capital letters it says "LARA IS BACK." Nothing, it seems, had changed. Gard articulated the issue in 1997: "I had problems when they started putting lower-cut clothes on her and sometimes taking her clothes off completely. It's really weird when you see a character of yours doing these things. You can't believe it. You think 'She can't do that!' I've spent my life drawing pictures of things and they're mine, you know? They belong to me."

# WILDFLOWERS

In the nineties, Music Television tried its first non-music program, *The Real World*. The MTV program was, to paraphrase the show's opening credits, when seven strangers are picked to live in a house to show what happens when people stop being polite and start being real. It was a big risk for a channel known only for music videos, but *The Real World* gained high enough ratings to return with a new cast.

In one of the second season's episodes, Jon, an eighteen year old virgin and country singer never seen without his 10-gallon hat, is sitting with his television roommate Dave, a struggling African-American comedian reminiscent of Eddie Murphy in both looks and tone. Dave's beeper goes off. "Do you sell drugs?" Jon asks with a grin. Dave scowls and lets him know that, with his ridiculous hat and southern Christian upbringing, he expected a racist assumption – that being black means you sell drugs – to come from his redneck mouth. Jon blinks several times. "I'm making a joke! Didn't you ever see the first season of *The Real World* when Heather's beeper goes off and (white) Julie asks (black) Heather if she sells drugs?" Dave, perhaps embarrassed for his tirade, just gives Jon the middle finger. In the previous season, Julie, Heather, and the other five strangers picked to live in a SoHo house may have had no idea what would happen to them (MTV claims the participants weren't prepped at all) or who their roommates were before everyone moved in, but they certainly did not know they would have the heated conflicts about sex, racism and class, budding romance between roommates, near fisticuffs and, perhaps most importantly, how these few recorded months of their life would forever define them to an audience of millions. *The Real World* was the first major American reality television show. Jon, David and the other season two roommates were likely part of this audience of millions, knowing enough about the show to want to get involved, and were probably aware of what would or could happen while the cameras were rolling. Like *The Real World* fans, they knew whatever they did in that house would forever be caught on tape. Jon's referential joke revealed that this spontaneous, real life journey that he and the other cast members were supposedly partaking actually had precedence. Reality TV was becoming self aware.

The Real World's first season cast featured a rough-edged, heavy-set female rapper, a grunge-era thin man with curly, greasy hair, a goth-pale Midwestern hipster and, with the exception of a male underwear model, three other non-photogenic people. They were average. The only requirement seemed to be participants being between eighteen and twenty five. It would be a surprise hit, earning MTV some of its highest ratings yet. The show managed to capture the elusive, yet influential 18 – 24 year old demographic, which made it attractive to advertisers. The network launched *Road Rules*, which would best be described as *The Real World* on wheels, and it began scaling back music videos in favor of reality programming. MTV would produce almost twenty *The Real World* seasons within the next fifteen years. Participants in the second season were nearly as average as the first, but the roommates seemed to become thinner and prettier with each new cast. Eventually the standard women were a size 2 or 4, often buxom. More than a handful would go on to pose in *Playboy*. The men were chiseled Adonises, easy on the eyes and a little dangerous. Originally a bunch of bike messengers and aspiring artists, *The Real World* actors became fashion models or aspiring actors in following seasons. (One participant even admitted that the experience would look good on her acting reel.) The first *The Real World* season was like the average college dorm, highlighted by late-night political discussion, awkward conversations and occasional partying. A decade later, during season twelve, roommates had a threesome in the first episode in the MTV-provided hot tub. Defending their questionable behavior on the show, cast members would later suggest MTV encouraged them to act wild on camera. The network kept a steady open bar in the house and at every club they visited. Some claimed the MTV crew would pull them aside and ask probing, passive-aggressive questions off camera, such as "We heard Jon say he likes the Confederate flag. How does that make you feel?"

CBS' producers fueled antagonism with participants on *Survivor*, the first major situation-based reality television show. Launched in May 2000, the series threw a dozen people on a deserted island. Each person was forced to find food and participate in physical "tribal challenges." People would get voted off the island – one by one – by other contestants. The last person standing received a one million dollar cash prize. Like *The Real World*'s first season, *Survivor* participants had to feel their way through different, new situations. For instance, how do you cook a rat you just caught (or, more pointedly, is that a rat you just caught)? On some level the audience knew the island wasn't deserted, as there were obviously cameras everywhere, and perhaps even that there were hamburgers, hot dogs and other traditional modern foods on the island, since the cameramen, the light guy, the host, Jeff Probst, and other CBS crew had to eat, too. Millions of viewers seemed happy to suspend disbelief. It became the number one program on regular television.

"In the Nintendo age, we expect our televised entertainment to take a new form: a series of competitive tests, growing more challenging over time," Steven Johnson writes in *Everything Bad Is Good For You*. Soon there were programs like ABC's *Joe Millionaire*, where women would compete to marry who they thought was a rich stranger, to NBC's *Fear Factor*, in which people would win prizes by successfully eating live scorpions, bungie jumping off a cliff or other dares. *Big Brother* put several people in an isolated, cramped house and voted the most annoying people out. *The Swan* took several so-called "ugly ducklings" and paid for a totally makeover, including extensive plastic surgery. The most improved would get a prize. "Reality shows cost anywhere from a quarter to half as much to produce as scripted shows," Michael Hirschorn, VH1 Executive Vice President of Original Programming and Production, acknowledged in *The Atlantic Monthly*. "Even television programmers see the genre as a kind of visual Hamburger Helper: cheap filler that saves them money they can use elsewhere for more-worthy programming." Hamburger Helper would eventually become more than a fifth of all TV programming. Following *Survivor*'s model, most would feature a bunch of competitive strangers that are confined to a limited area and are slowly picked off week after week. And like *The Real World*, any season two participants would be more aware than the previous bunch: more aware of the cameras, the limelight and the repercussions. It wasn't necessarily about reality anymore, but about watching beautiful people in simulated situations and observing them as one might a hamster in a well-greased wheel.

Wil Wright released his people simulation, *The Sims*, in February 2000, about three months before *Survivor* first aired. According to the book *Smartbomb*, Wright once sat down and talked to a group of twelve year olds about the game. The first question they asked was if you could kill your character. The question didn't disturb the lanky, brilliant designer at all. "[Wright] says the kids were doing the most natural thing in the world: trying to intuit the boundaries of the possibility space they were given – 'That's a kid's job,' he says." Wright's previous game was *SimAnt*.

■ ■ ■

*The Sims* is a simple game. You create a human character, or Sim, which can be made into your or someone else's likeness, or into a random, imaginary person. You can take a prefab home or design an original house using a basic toolkit. Your Sim is then plopped into an imaginary house in American suburbia alongside other, computer-controlled Sims that play your neighbors. The game is spent making sure your Sim is happy by maintaining its eight ratings: bladder, comfort, energy, fun, hunger, hygiene, room and social. While it is possible to complete pointed tasks and minigames, there is no end to *The Sims*. Your little person is living a life. It is always there.

There were two early inspirations for *The Sims*. The first was Tamagotchi, a children's toy released by Japanese game developer Bandai in 1996. It was a small locket with a digital display of an egg. When you turn on the device for the first time, it hatches. Most of them resemble a rat with big ears. As owner of a brand new Tamagotchi, your job is to press a button and feed the baby whenever it became hungry, which, on average, is every half-hour. (It also slept.) Millions of Tamagotchis were sold, bootleg and otherwise.

The second inspiration for *The Sims* was a generally forgotten Commodore 64 game, *Raid on Bungling Bay*, which was Wright's first title. In the action game, you fly a chunky helicopter over pixilated terrain and try to destroy everything that moves. It was a minor hit. Wright admits that *Raid on Bungling Bay* was a "dumb game." Like many game creators, he made design software so he could produce new *Raid on Bungling Bay* levels quickly. He'd shuffle the pre-made tiles around, laying down bridges, buildings and bodies of water where he pleased. This part was fun, he thought, later telling *The*

*New Yorker* he "was more interested in creating the buildings on the islands than in blowing them up."

After studying several books on urban dynamics, Wright created a city simulator based on his game design tool. You could make buildings, organize city power and strategically map residential and commercial districts, but you also had to monitor crime, watch the city budget and keep the populous happy. He added a natural disaster icon that featured a giant, fire-breathing lizard. And, unlike most video games, you could play as long as you liked. There was no end. Broderbund, the publisher of *Raid on Bungling Bay*, said it didn't see the point in a game you couldn't beat. It passed. Two years later Wright met Jeff Braun, a Silicon Valley entrepreneur, and showed him what he now called *SimCity*. The two started their own company, Maxis, and released the game in 1989. The company was based in Braun's apartment. Through word of mouth, Maxis' *SimCity* became a cult favorite and spawned several back-to-back sequels including *SimCity 2000*, *SimEarth* and *SimAnt*. Electronic Arts, purchased Maxis and gave Wright seventeen million dollars worth of EA shares for his portion of the company.

*The Sims* is a natural extension of *SimCity*. What happens when you zoom in on a group of people within a bustling city you control? It was the microcosm of the macrocosm. Wright poured over sociological theories such as Maslow's hierarchy, the theory that human needs can be prioritized in a five-step pyramid (physiological, safety, love/belonging, esteem and self-actualization), and books like E. O. Wilson's *The Ants*.

In an average day (in the game, not in real life), your Sim will wake up at a reasonable time in the morning (unless he or she had a late night out, in which case you need to wake your Sim at a reasonable time yourself). It will then stand there. If it has priorities adjusted towards, say, partying, it may walk over to the billiards table and play a game of pool (not that there is anything wrong with that at 6:00 a.m.). More than likely, however, after eight hours sleep or a long night of drinking, your Sim will have to go to the bathroom. It subtly begins jumping up and down, sometimes holding its crotch. You move the cursor to the bathroom (you did build a bathroom in the house, didn't you?) and tell the Sim to walk there. It moves. Once it gets there, you click on the new option, Use Bathroom. It pulls down its pants and squats on the toilet, the details covered in a fuzzy blur. After a minute (or two), the Sim gets up, turns around and flushes the toilet. You click on the sink and the Sim will wash its hands. The Sim is messy, so usually you will find several water spots on the tiled floor. You should find the closet, tell the Sim to walk there, click on the mop, tell the Sim to walk back to the bathroom, and then click on the appropriate wet tile squares (roughly 10 pixels across) for the Sim to mop them up. Your Sim could slip and fall and die if you're not careful with that. "What makes The Sims so popular is its dogged adherence to the minutiae of subsistence, and that's where we're supposed to feel the realism," wrote Chuck Klosterman in *Sex, Drugs and Cocoa Puffs: A Low Culture Manifesto*. He dedicated a whole chapter to the game. "The Sims make the unconscious conscious, but not in an existential Zen way; The Sims forces you to think about how even free people are eternally enslaved by the process of living. Suddenly, I had to remember to go to the bathroom. I had to *plan* to take a shower… And though I need to do all those things in reality, the thoughts scarcely cross my mind unless I'm plugged into the game."

It was released on the PC in 2000, the year that situation-based reality television began, and was an instant hit. In short time EA followed up with *The Sims: Livin' Large, The Sims: Hot Date, The Sims: House Party, The Sims Online, The Sims Deluxe, The Sims: Unleashed, The Sims: Vacation, The Sims* (Sony Playstation 2, Microsoft XBox and Nintendo GameCube editions), *The Sims: Superstar, The Sims: Bustin' Out, The Sims: Makin' Magic, The Urbs: Sims in the City, Sims: University, Sims: Nightlife, Sims: Open for Business* and *Sims: Seasons. The Sims 2* came out, too.

The Sims and its spinoffs sold 85 million copies, making it the top-selling commercial video game of all time. Hundreds, if not thousands of players designed personal websites for their *Sims*: day-in-the-life diaries (later called blogs), wedding web pages and, when animals were introduced to the series, pet sites. *Time* found one player who liked to "re-create real-life interpersonal relationships" in the game to see how things would play out. Other players would set up torture scenarios, like having their Sim eat several meals and then trap them in a closet and have them piss or shit on themselves and pass out from exhaustion on the feces-covered floor. Homemade Sims videos would be passed around the Internet. *Time* noted, "[I]n the hands of its legions of devotees, the game has become an expressive language they can use to

THE LARA CROFT ERA: WILDFLOWERS

tell stories about their own lives." Despite dozens of sequels and spinoffs, *The Sims* games remained focused on mundane tasks. Wright only provided blank characters that users could project their own values, prejudices and issues onto. He discussed his game, his experiment in *Smartbomb*. "It's gotten to the point now where I surf the fan sites everyday and download cool things the fans have created, which is really ironic in a way! Because now it's the fans out there that are entertaining us, the developers, with their creations!"

"Reality programming unfolds in the most artificial of environments… [b]ut they nonetheless possess an emotional authenticity that is responsible for much of their appeal," Steven Johnson says in *Everything Bad Is Good For You*. "At the peak moments – when Joe Millionaire reveals his true construction worker identity; when a contestant gets kicked off the island late in a *Survivor* series – the camera zooms in on the crestfallen face of the unlucky contestant, and what you see for a few fleeting seconds is something you almost never see in prime-time entertainment: a display of genuine emotion written on someone's face. The thrill of it is the thrill of something real and unplanned bursting out in the most staged and sterile of places, like a patch of wildflowers blooming in a parking lot."

■ ■ ■

When Electronic Arts released *The Sims Online*, the Internet itself had arguably reached its tipping point. "In its early years, consumers logged on at hyperspeed. U.S. households online soared from zero to about 50% in six years…," wrote *Business Week*. "PCs took 18 years to reach the same penetration." The average modem speed was 56 Kilobytes/per second, or 56 K, at least twice as fast as when the Sierra Network launched years earlier. Visually and structurally complex video games could be played over the Internet now that information was passed faster between computers. (America OnLine (AOL), which purchased The Sierra Network years earlier, was now by far the largest Internet service provider.) The first major online role playing game was 3DO's *Meridian 59*, released in 1995. A sword and sorcery game, *Meridian 59* is essentially a visual version of the classic *Dungeons & Dragons*-inspired text adventures like *MUD*. The designers reportedly established the term massively multiplayer online role playing game, or MMORPG. It won several industry awards, but became a cult classic rather than an outright hit.

EA's first foray into MMORPGs was *Ultima Online* in 1997. The creator was Richard Garriott, the same designer who made a fortune with his small company, Origin, in the early '80s. After his hit *Akalabeth: World of Doom*, Garriott started a popular series of role playing games called *Ultima*. *Ultima Online* would be an Internet-enabled version of the long-standing world, Britannia. It would have its own currency, economy and weather. The non-player characters, or NPCs, including barnyard animals and gruesome monsters, would have their own artificial intelligence. It would be a fully-functional online world. It garnered more than 250,000 subscribers. "The first time I visited Britannia, I went as Gudrun, a young archer," journalist Elizabeth Kolbert wrote in *The New Yorker*. "I gave her a peaches-and-cream complexion, blond pigtails, and a not very medieval miniskirt. Not long after Gudrun arrived in the kingdom, she met Dark Wolf. Dark Wolf was wearing a red robe and carrying a long sword. He bought Gudrun some shoes, and also a suit of leather armor, which, when she put it on, turned out to be a tight-fitting affair halfway between a cuirass and a bustier. It was unclear to me whether Dark Wolf was expressing simple fellow-feeling for Gudrun or something harder to satisfy." Kolbert's article was titled "Pimps & Dragons." In *Sex in Video Games*, Garriott said sex-related services began in the game immediately after it went live. "Two people had logged into the game and one person was 'pimping' for the other, who would then lead people into a storeroom along the docks where they hung out and 'ooh and ah' at the 'John.' The game supported no depictions of sex, but the player 'demand' was clearly present, and they engineered their own solution." Any of the quarter million players could pass by the docks and, if they wanted to, stop and watch.

# CLOSETS

On the night of March 11, 2000, a group of fraternity guys were drunk and angry. They just spent two hours watching the Ellen DeGeneres-produced lesbian drama *If These Walls Could Talk 2* and not seen any "hot lesbian sex." In a non-sequitur that would become typical of *Saturday Night Live*, one of the frat boys, played by comedian Jimmy Fallon, says he has a genie that can grant him three wishes. He uses the first two wishes on important things, like turning their small beer keg into a larger beer keg, and then decides to use the last wish to make two lesbians appear in the room and start making out. He asks that the women be unaware they are watching. His wish is granted and the two women appear in his bed, but they immediately realize something is wrong. Both women are homely-looking, wearing heavy flannel clothing and homemade cut-off shorts, and the hair on their legs seems longer than the hair on their heads. The frat starts complaining to the genie, but she explains that the wish cannot be taken back. The lesbians embrace. One lover licks the other one's face. A frat boy puts his head behind the couch and starts vomiting. Another one starts crying something to the effect of "These aren't real lesbians!" A third shouts "This thing is giving me a hard-*off!*"

A few years earlier, Ellen DeGeneres decided that the character she played in her popular ABC sitcom, *Ellen*, would come out of the closet. In other words, the character, also named Ellen, would reveal she was gay. DeGeneres herself had not publicly discussed her own sexuality, despite rumors that she was a lesbian. "Outing" her self-named sitcom character would out her in the process. The year before, the Walt Disney Company purchased the American Broadcast Company. Executives at the parent company were against DeGeneres' idea. Once word leaked on the potential episode, ABC affiliates across the Bible Belt said they would not air the show. Long-time advertisers bailed. In the end, ABC executives decided to do the episode. "Times have changed," CNN said of the heavily watched episode. "ABC lost $1 million in advertising revenue when the *thirtysomething* show depicted two gay men in bed. Seven years later, there are sponsors for *Ellen* and they reportedly paid more than $300,000 for each 30-second spot." *Time* gave DeGeneres the cover. It read, "Yep, I'm Gay".

One of the most critically noted movies at the time was *Bound*, a bloody crime caper starring a effeminate, busty character played by Jennifer Tilly and a hard-driving plumber played by Gina Gershon. They were lovers in the film. Several cultural critics wrote about the sexual tension in *Thelma and Louise*, the Geena Davis and Susan Sarandon movie in which two women kill a rapist, but found the lesbian undercurrent symbolic, not literal. Catherine Tramell, Sharon Stone's character in *Basic Instinct*, kissed her lesbian girlfriend throughout the film, but Tramell herself was a bisexual. *Basic Instinct* focused on the dynamics between her and the male lead, Michael Douglas. There are only two leads in 1996's *Bound*: lesbians Violet and Corky. Andy and Larry Wachowski, who would later write and direct *The Matrix*, even hired expert Susie Bright as their on-set sex consultant. *Bound* is about the lovers' plan to steal two million dollars from Violet's mafia boyfriend, Caesar. Corky is an ex-con, a former professional thief, which is why Violet asks for her help. They only know each other from a one-night stand the evening before. Corky explains her reservations to Violet. "For me, stealing has always been a lot like sex. Two people who want the same thing. They get in a room, they talk about it. They start to plan. It's kind of like flirting. It's kind of like... foreplay. Because the more they talk about it, the wetter they get." Corky gives a sly smile and readjusts in her seat. "The only difference is I can fuck someone I've just met. But to steal, I need to know someone like I know myself." Violet coaxes her into getting involved, but the plan goes awry and Caesar catches them, traps them in his bedroom and ties them up in heavy rope. The mobster points his gun at Corky. He interrogates her on the location of the money. Then he demands to know how she stole "his woman." "Everybody knows your kind can't be trusted. Fuckin' queers. You make me sick... What did you do to her, huh?" He is practically salivating. "What did you fuckin' do to her? That's not my Violet!" He turns and points the gun at his girlfriend. "What did she do to you?" Violet looks at him coolly. "Everything you couldn't." Caesar leans back, lets out a heavy sigh and turns his back to them. Caesar has murdered several people to find out where his money is, including a mafia boss, but at this point he seems ready to give up. The gun may as well be shooting blanks.

"Corky had to be the kind of woman whom everyone in the theater would be dying to go to bed with…" Susie Bright later wrote in her book *Mommy's Little Girl*. "Violet, on the other hand, couldn't be just any straight girl on the drift. She had to be a femme diva, as calculating and as sensual as a cat."

In the first scene of the 2001 video game *Fear Effect 2: Retro Helix*, Hana, a curvy, short-haired brunette, is entering what looks like a pay-by-the-hour motel. The camera zooms in on her behind, taking in her semi-translucent black negligee and white thong panties. She slinks towards the john sitting at the bed's edge. He is blond and buff, and wears a childish, ear-to-ear grin. Hana moves in front of the nameless man and slowly begins taking off her dark nightie. The room dims. Later that evening, Hana walks into the bathroom and looks down at her lover in the bathtub. He is now dead, his lifeless body bobbing in the bloody water. She notices that he's wearing the same grin his face, which makes her smile. She has to ask. "So, was it worth dying for?"

■ ■ ■

Stanley Liu, creator of the *Fear Effect* series, was raised in Hong Kong. To make sure he blended in with the other boys, his father let him drink beer at age four and gave him cigarettes as a teenager. "When you take away the taboo of things, it becomes a non-issue," Liu would later say. In 1988, the Chinese government would create a movie rating system, the highest being "sai chai," or category IV, equal to an X rating. Liu was in Hong Kong in the late sixties and early seventies, well before the more liberal ratings. He wouldn't see his first porn movie until he was 16, when he came to America. "When I was in Hong Kong, there was no such thing as a XXX movie – the law said they can't show intercourse and nothing below the waist, something like that. The worst I was were some breast shots!" he said. "They were more restrictive. *Very* conservative with sex." He says his viewpoint was further complicated by religious views. "My parents are hardcore Buddhists. However, I was sent to a British Catholic school through most of my young adult life. I grew up with this clash of Chinese superstition and Western Catholicism in my head. I remember vividly how we had to burn offerings to our ancestors in July and make Sunday mass at the same time."

Liu attended the Art Center in Southern California to study digital graphic art. After graduating he did cinematic effects for major video game companies like Origin, creator of the popular role playing series *Ultima*, and Sierra, of *Leisure Suit Larry* fame. (He did not work on the Al Lowe series.) Liu then pooled his resources and started his own game company, Kronos Digital Entertainment. The small, boutique developer would make games other publishers would distribute. Japanese publisher Vic Tokai sold its first title, the 3D fighting game *Criticom*, in late 1995. It followed up with *Dark Rift*. "*Dark Rift* is the product of Kronos, the same company responsible for the abysmal Playstation fighter *Criticom*," the website *GameSpot* wrote. "While *Dark Rift* isn't a sequel, the lackluster fighting contained on the cart might as well have been culled from a mythical realm called *Criticom II*. On the upside, *Dark Rift* isn't quite as bad as *Criticom*." It received a 5 out of 10. Most major reviewers echoed *GameSpot's* opinion, though some thought the graphics in *Dark Rift* were impressive.

All the while, Liu dreamt of creating an aggressive, gun-happy animated movie similar to the popular Asian action flicks he grew up watching. He was a big fan of John Woo, the Hong Kong director of *Hard Boiled*, *The Killer* and other violent, critically-acclaimed action films. Liu and his business partner, John Zuur Patten, talked about paying homage to anime, a Japanese animation style that usually focuses on surreal settings, strong female protagonists and violent resolutions. One of the most famous was 1988's *Akira*. Liu's movie would star a group of ruthless Western bounty hunters led by a headstrong femme fatale named Hana. Their exploits would lead them straight into a mythological Chinese hell. "The whole concept of Hell and life after death was always an interesting philosophical mind twister to me," Liu said in a interview. "When I came up with the concept and the back-story for *Fear Effect*, it was like… therapy!" *Fear Effect* for the Sony PlayStation (PSOne) would balance highly challenging action-adventure levels with anime-inspired animated shorts called cutscenes. Liu wanted to blend the player-controlled portions and the cutscenes well enough so that the two would be almost indistinguishable. Previous home games like Tecmo's *Ninja Gaiden* had an obvious distinction between the interactive and the cinematic. Arcade games like Cinematronic's classic *Dragon's Lair* were smooth, but required expensive hardware to run. "We had to make sure that the cinematics and gameplay were seamless," Liu said. "I mean, the label 'interactive movie' is a death sentence."

The last notable interactive movie was Sega's *Night Trap*, a 1992 game that used digital footage. It featured several teenage girls having a slumber party, discussing boys and other important matters, while vampires, who resemble men with stockings on their heads, quietly hunt down the girls with what looks to be a long drill. Your job is to defend the helpless women. Pressing a button at the right time would show a vampire being caught in one of the many set traps, while bad timing would show prerecorded footage of girls being subdued in some angry, PG-level way. The girls tended to disperse. To do the job right, you have to constantly watch footage of the women from hidden cameras stationed in every room. *Night Trap* had no nudity, but the panty-raiding voyeurism created a minor controversy. One of the "teenagers" featured was Dana Plato, the actress who played Kimberly Drummond on the eighties sitcom *Diff'rent Strokes*. That same year she would star in *Bikini Beach Race*, a porn with Ron Jeremy.

Quality issues aside, Liu realized that home game system technology had advanced since *Night Trap*. The Sony PSOne used high-memory CDs instead of low-memory cartridges, which allowed programmers to include visuals less grainy than in *Night Trap*. *Fear Effect* could have more storage space to showcase the game world. Developers could also spread a game across multiple CDs, something not possible with cartridges. Kronos determined *Fear Effect* would span four separate discs, one for each of the game's worlds. Also in Kronos' favor was a competitor's title, *Resident Evil*. Capcom's zombie horror series, which balanced B-movie thrills with action sequences, would eventually sell more than 24 million copies. It even coined a new game genre: survival horror. While not as visually stunning as the game Liu proposed, *Resident Evil* proved that a great story could be told while still keeping the gameplay solid. Kronos talked with potential *Fear Effect* distributors, including *Tomb Raider* publisher Eidos. "It was an uphill battle. I even had to convince some of our in-house people that the game was viable," he said. "I remember being in the boardroom after the Eidos presentation of the first game and, afterwards, the president looked me straight in the eye and said 'How much of this is just cool in your head, Stan?'"

Eidos did eventually give Kronos a deal and released *Fear Effect* in February 2000. One review read: "From out [of] nowhere, it seems, comes Kronos, who hasn't made a single game that's worth owning, until today. *Fear Effect* won't knock *Resident Evil* off the survival horror map, but it takes the *Resident Evil* formula and prods and pushes it in new shapes and directions like a kid with Play Dough." One major point of interest was the *Fear Effect's* domineering leader, Hana. She wore tight, revealing outfits throughout the game. In interviews, Liu was often asked if there was a code you could punch in to play Hana nude, an understandable question with the rumors that a similar was available for another Eidos game, *Tomb Raider*. Liu said no. "You get to see Hana in her bare minimum quite a bit throughout the game. For me, it is more interesting to see her in different sexy outfits than it is to see her in her raw, exposed nakedness. We got some very interesting costumes designed for her next endeavor. Rest assured, there will be plenty left for the imagination."

An unprecedented success, Kronos immediately went to work on a *Fear Effect* sequel. The team knew it wanted to add more of whatever made the original a hit: more background story, more violence, more sex appeal. Kronos used new graphic techniques to get more visual detail out of the aging PSOne system. It gave the sequel an easier learning curve, to make it more accessible than the original, and provided thirteen possible endings to the game based on what decisions you made. Hana also got a lover. Her name was Rain. "A lot of subject matters, like homosexuality, are brought up in our game not to shock, piss off or offend anyone, but to look and talk about it. Video games are a great medium and, now that many game players are grown-up adults, to restrict it is such a waste. So, Hana's sexual preference wasn't made to put people into shock, but because it fit her character," Liu said. In one cutscene, the two bounty hunters need to assassinate someone, but first they must distract the building guards to use a secret elevator. After a quick discussion, Hana grabs her busty blonde companion and starts making out with her in the small shaft. Hana begins to peel her tight green party dress off, but stops just before getting naked. She waggles a free finger at the camera. "Sorry, boys. This is private," she says, tossing her dress over the surveillance equipment to block the view. Two male guards are watching in the camera room. "Damn. Should we kick 'em out?" one asks. "No way!" the other replies. "Maybe the dress will fall off!" In an early action sequence, Rain has been taken hostage by a multi-tentacle alien. The monster has stolen Rain's clothes and strapped her into four-point restraints located in its laboratory. (The scene is similar to Jabba the Hutt capturing Princess Leia and dressing her in a metal bikini in *Return of the Jedi*.) In the battle, you use Hana to fight the alien while Rain writhes and squirms, struggling against the cold metal restraints, wearing nothing more than her bra and panties." Originally, we heard a 'tone it down' speech from Eidos, because Wal-Mart wouldn't carry *Fear Effect 2: Retro Helix* if it was too explicit," Liu recalled. "I'd say by mid-production, though, we said 'Screw it!' And it stayed. We have a little touching and such, but it all fits in the story."

Eidos began an extensive *Fear Effect 2: Retro Helix* print campaign in Winter 2000, the same time it started promoting the fourth *Tomb Raider* game, *The Last Revelation*. In the two-page spread, Rain is straddling Hana, and Hana is lying on her stomach reading a magazine called *Big Guns*. They are both in their underwear. Referring to *Fear Effect 2*'s multiple endings, the caption reads "No one's surprised this story is capable of thirteen climaxes". *GamePro* refused to run the ad, as did other publications with a younger-skewing readership. Eidos provided them with a more acceptable ad. "The original ad had no explicit nudity, just light touching and innuendos, but they had a problem with the word 'climax,'" Liu said. "We have another ad where Hana and Rain are in regular clothing that says 'These two ladies put the ass in assassin'. And that one's OK!" Men's magazines like *Stuff* happily ran the original ad. The hipster sex magazine *Nerve* profiled the *Fear Effect* women in a photo spread, guns drawn, along with quotes from Liu about the elevator make out scene. *Playboy.com* did an article on the advertising controversy. Eidos provided different *Fear Effect 2* ads based on the country. The Italian ad was similar to America's censored one, with the text "Don't let us play on our own." The German advertisement had Hana and Rain partially naked, giving each other a hug as they look at the reader. Rain is wearing virgin white bra and panties, while Hana is clad in the same black nightie and white thongs she wore in the game's murderous cutscene introduction. The women have guns in hand. A caption reads, in big brown letters, "*Stell dir vor, du hast eine uzi und eine pumpgun... und einen verdammt geilen arsch!*" Roughly: "Imagine you have an Uzi and a shotgun... and a damned hot ass!"

Eidos released *Fear Effect 2: Retro Helix* for the PSOne in February 2001, a year after the original game. It received excellent ratings. The tough magazine *NextGen* made *Fear Effect 2* the featured review of the month, giving it four-and-a-half out of five stars. Critics said graphically it pushed the Sony PSOne as far as it could go. Three months earlier, in November 2000, Sony launched its advanced PlayStation 2 (PS2). Kronos began working on *Fear Effect 3: Inferno* for the new system. The PS2 would allow bigger games because it used DVDs instead of CDs, similar to how CDs were a big leap from cartridges. "The first two games raised a lot of questions we plan to wrap up in [part three]," Liu said in a 2001 interview. "A lot of technical problems came because the first two games had to be on four CDs, so with [*Fear Effect*] 3 being on DVD, we hope to not have as much constraint." Kronos and Eidos attended the Electronic Entertainment Expo, the largest American video game conference, to show a two-minute collage of cutscenes from the upcoming game. In one scene, Hana is running down the hallway of an asylum while being chased by aggressive hospital guards. They trap her in a corner and pull out a needle, presumably filled with medicine that will sedate her. In a panic, Hana scratches one of the guards and his whole face falls off, revealing bloody muscles and long fangs. She manages to escape into an elevator and, as she takes a deep breath, the elevator walls begin to ooze blood. The preview showed a level a gore well beyond anything in the first two games. The following year, *Fear Effect: Inferno* was a no show at the annual gaming conference. Eidos tells the press that the game is "on hold at the current time". In short time Eidos says the project is "indefinitely postponed". Stanley Liu and his company Kronos were no longer available for comment. Calls to the offices were answered by a disconnected phone line message. Several sources say that the members of Kronos went their separate ways and all game-related assets had been destroyed. Eccentric movie director Uwe Boll, best known for the 2003 flop based on Sega's *House of the Dead*, bought the film and TV rights to *Fear Effect*. "*Fear Effect* is a fantastic game with a dark story," he said in a press release. "I want to create an action film in the vein of *Charlie's Angels*, but portray its sexy heroines Hana and Rain in a much edgier fashion."

■ ■ ■

In 2000, Showtime cable channel started *Queer As Folk*, the first major gay soap opera. *Will & Grace*, an NBC comedy about a gay man and his straight female friend, was a top-five prime time hit. MTV launched the gay-focused cable channel Logo. Another new basic cable channel, Bravo, began several gay-friendly shows, including *Queer Eye for the Straight Guy*, a makeover program where five gay men help a hapless straight man improve his couture, grooming, decorating, cooking and social skills. The so-called fab five appeared on the cover of *Entertainment Weekly*, cut an official single and video for its theme song "All Things (Just Keep Getting Better)" and, perhaps the biggest pop cultural measurement at the time, were parodied on the satirical cartoon *South Park*. Showtime launched the lesbian drama *The L Word*, which became another hit for the network. Unlike most pornographic films or mainstream movies, these programs were not created or written by straight males, but by people intimately familiar with the cultures. Based on Nielsen ratings and cable data, millions of Americans were watching gay and lesbian-focused shows, letting a previously unknown subculture into their living room as easily as they observed the four straight single women on HBO's popular *Sex And The City*.

By the time *Fear Effect 3* was lost in indefinite postponement, websites such as *GayGamer.net* were representing the gay and lesbian video game community. Players were affectionately called gaymers. A Nottingham Trent University study at the time found that 54 percent of male gamers and 68 percent of female gamers preferred to create game avatars, or online personas, of the opposite sex – women to avoid "unsolicited male approaches" and men because they found themselves being treated better by other male players. Just a decade earlier, Nintendo refused to allow Capcom to release its seminal arcade brawler *Final Fight* on its Super Nintendo system. In the fighting game you beat up drugged-out street urchins, Mafia bosses and crooked cops. You also defend yourself against two women, Roxy and Poison. Depending on the version of the game, the two sisters have long pink or purple hair, tiny cut-off shorts and half t-shirts that barely hold their breasts. Handcuffs hang from their shorts. Their tight t-shirts rise when you hit them. According to *Game Over: Nintendo's Battle*

*To Dominate Videogames*, the game company told Capcom abuse against women was against its content policies. Capcom told Nintendo that Roxy and Poison weren't always women. They were transgender. *Final Fight* was released on the Super Nintendo in 1991 – sans Roxy and Poison. (A rare home port, for the Sega CD, reportedly has the sisters. Later Capcom games would feature them in less revealing attire.) The topic was discussed enough for *Street Fighter IV* producer Yoshinori Ono to explain Poison's gender years later. "In North America, Poison is officially a post-op transsexual. But in Japan, she simply tucks her business away in order to look like a girl."

Atari, which now only released games, not systems, published *Dungeons & Dragons: The Temple of Elemental Evil*. Based on the popular pen-and-paper games from the 1970s, *The Temple of Elemental Evil* was a role playing title geared towards hardcore gamers. In one point in an otherwise straightforward game, you and your merry party of men met a slave named Bertram. The slave says that if you can defeat his master, he'll repay you by marrying a male party member. Beat Bertram's master and you're treated to a wholesome same sex marriage ceremony. "And Elemental Evil isn't the only place where gamers can find gay romance," tech journalist Clive Thompson wrote on the website *Slate*. "Players of *Knights of the Old Republic* discovered that while playing a female Jedi, they get hit on by another female Jedi. Later this year, virtual gay wedlock will hit the mainstream when The Sims 2, the long-awaited sequel to the most popular PC title of all time, allows marriages between same-sex Sims."

The Sims 2 became the first major American video game to allow gay marriages, but the series had always allowed gay couples. There were no press releases. No special *The Sims: Gay Edition*. You just made your Sim flirt with someone of the same sex and build a relationship from there. "The inclusion of gay relationships in The Sims and other games reflects the Will & Grace effect," said *Wired* sex and technology critic Regina Lynn. "For the majority of the gamer generation, there's nothing more provocative, political or puerile about homosexuality in The Sims – it's simply no big deal." This may have been easier to swallow since *The Sims* had no on-screen sex. (Later editions, such as *The Sims: Hot Date*, introduced heavy petting.) When the Internet-connected *The Sims Online* was released, the gay magazine *The Advocate* wrote that the game had the potential to "bust down antigay

THE LARA CROFT ERA: CLOSETS

barriers around the globe." When *The Advocate* asked one of the game designers about the inclusion, he responded that "[o]ur decision was not to put artificial limits on behavior. We're here to make games, not push any moral agenda, so [allowing gay Sims] seemed like a no-brainer."

The first major moment in online gay gaming didn't happen with Sims people, however, but among elves and orcs. While *The Sims Online* came and went, 100 players gathered in a major virtual city, put on their digital pink shirts and staged the first virtual gay pride parade in *World of Warcraft*, the largest massive multiplayer online role playing game (MMORPG). The parade was prompted by Sara Andrews, a transgender woman from Nashville. She wanted to create a LGBT-friendly (lesbian, gay, bisexual and transgender) club within the *WoW* universe. Anti-gay slurs tended to fly faster under the anonymity of a computer screen. It was not unusual for established virtual worlds to have gay-friendly cliques for comradely playing. *WoW* developer Blizzard Entertainment told Andrews she couldn't create the club and, if she used the LGBT acronym within the game, her *WoW* account would be canceled. In a later statement, Blizzard said its goal was to "promote a positive game environment for everyone and help prevent... harassment from taking place." Lambda Legal Defense, America's biggest LGBT rights organization, joined Andrew's cause. Lambda announced a potential lawsuit, *WoW* players organized a gay pride parade and Blizzard retracted its decision all in about three weeks.

In the first two years more than six million players joined *World of Warcraft*, and in those 700 days Blizzard's duty switched from providing fresh dungeons and monsters to managing the social dynamics of a world more populated than Los Angeles. After the pink parade, the legal threat and the bad press, Blizzard Entertainment called the club rejection "a misunderstanding" and said it would give more sensitivity training to the online game managers – the modern day Dungeon Masters – monitoring the everyday happenings of the virtual world. Talking to the *San Francisco Bay Times*, a Blizzard spokesperson told people not to expect a miracle. "We can't do everything," she said. "It's a very big world."

**PORN AND PONG**

# THE GRAND THEFT AUTO ERA
## (2001 – 2008)

*Grand Theft Auto*'s impact on new millennium culture is astonishing, especially when you realize the game is quite old: the first version came out in 1997. It took several iterations, a graphic upgrade and a mountain of controversy to ascend to 2001's landmark *Grand Theft Auto III*.

Mentioning *Tomb Raider* leads to only one thought – the curvy Lara Croft – but bringing up *Grand Theft Auto* unravels a complete world of car sex with prostitutes, virtual blowjobs from in-game girlfriends, and (now) illegal pornographic diversions uncovered like hidden gems. The louder the protests from Senator Hillary Clinton, conservative lawyer Jack Thompson and other public figures, the more real this game world became. Now they were debating the politics of virtual sex work as if at some town hall meeting.

*Grand Theft Auto* also served as a wonderful precursor to the "real" online hookups happening in game-inspired virtual worlds like *Second Life*, though in these cases there was actually another human at the other end. From a player standpoint, however, the sexual Turing test didn't seem to matter – you had a virtual fuck buddy either way.

This point is driven home when, in 2004, *Playboy* starts an annual spread of *naked video game characters*. The longtime cultural trendsetter of male sexual norms is now leaning on Microsoft, Sony and Rockstar Games to tell them what is sexy. In the Grand Theft Auto Era, games are no longer mimicking other mediums. Games are shaping them.

# FRANKENSTEIN

The 9/11 attacks on September 11, 2001, crushed four planes, two skyscrapers, one government building and 3,000 lives, but the terrorist run served an equally paralyzing blow to our cultural expression. On September 29, New York Mayor Rudolph Giuliani opened *Saturday Night Live*, the 30-year-old comedy show known for its biting social commentary. Bracketed by real New York firefighters and policemen, Giuliani had a serious opening monologue declaring that New York was still "open for business," but it would be weeks, if not months before any *Saturday Night Live* skits actually referenced the suffocating smoke, dead bodies and smoldering cinders still stewing down the street from its Manhattan studios. Sony withdrew a trailer from its new movie, *Spider-Man*, because it featured a helicopter caught in a web between the Trade Center towers. The soon-to-be-released Arnold Schwarzenegger vehicle *Collateral Damage* was held for more than a year because it revolved around a skyscraper bomb plot. *The New Yorker* wrote that violent, explosive Hollywood blockbusters seemed strange after we watched a live show, on 9/11, that was all too real. As America sifted through the psychological rubble, Rockstar Games released *Grand Theft Auto III*, a darkly sexual, anarchistic fairytale. It would become a lightning rod for our hopes and our fears in a way no other cultural expression on no other medium could be.

The beginnings of Rockstar Games, and of *Grand Theft Auto* specifically, were humble. The series was created by a bespectacled, unassuming Scotsman named David Jones. As a teenager he got a job working from Timex which, in Western European countries, was known for its computers as well as its watches. Its Sinclair series, including the Sinclair ZX Spectrum and Sinclair ZX81, became the home computer standard across Europe in the mid-'80s around the same time the IBM PC and Commodore 64 found popularity in the states. After four years, Jones left Timex and studied programming at the University of Abertay Dundee in Scotland. He found he was a natural at it. "I wondered if I could design a decent computer game in all this spare time," he would later say. Jones started a small company, DMA Designs, and created two games. He sold the second one, *Lemmings*, to Psygnosis, a well-established European publisher. In *Lemmings*, you direct a group of absent-minded, half-blind rodents from one end of the screen to the other while protecting them from high cliffs, blazing fires and other deadly dangers. Released in February 1991, *Lemmings* became one of the bestselling computer games of the decade. It was ported to roughly two dozen different game systems. It was also true to the creator: The sadomasochistic setup, to keep (or to not keep) cute animals from killing themselves, was reflective of Jones' own dark humor.

After the success of *Lemmings*, Jones expanded his development team and began working on a cop and robbers game called *Race 'n' Chase*. The goal was to create a living, breathing city with moving subway cars, commuters going to work and actual stoplights. It would have a 2D overhead view. DMA Designs successfully made a functional city, but decided to scrap most of the details that would be inconsequential to game play, such as the traffic lights. International music publisher BMG just launched its interactive entertainment arm and agreed to publish *Race 'n' Chase*, but only if it got a visual overhaul. The game's flat birds-eye perspective didn't look as sophisticated as 3D games for Sony's new system, the PlayStation (PSOne). The team spent another eighteen months recreating the now-dated 2D graphic engine from scratch. Though it kept the same viewpoint, DMA Designs used a special visual technique to give depth. In real life, if you are on a moving train and look out towards a forest, the trees nearest to you will appear to pass faster than those farther away. This, among other factors, shows you if an object is near or far. In *Race 'n' Chase*, the design team would make rooftops, overhead bridges and other high objects pass faster than the busy street action below. Parallax scrolling was popularized in 1989's *Shadow of the Beast*, a visually stunning action game released by *Lemmings* publisher Psygnosis. Not quite flat and not quite dynamic, designers would call the *Race 'n' Chase* viewpoint "two-d and a half."

While reworking the graphic engine, the developers noticed a major design problem. "No one wanted to play the cops," Jones recalled. Team member Brian Baglow added "If traffic was heavy you, as a cop, couldn't decide to drive on the sidewalk, or plough through a busy park. We couldn't let the player do that and reward them." Instead, *Race 'n' Chase* would reward you for being the best criminal possible. After answering a pay phone in the public park, your nameless main character would get various assignments, such as driving the getaway car after a bank job or offing a disloyal gang member. You could also *not* answer the pay phone and go on your own personal adventure, like stealing a car, running over a cop and shooting up a neighborhood park. There were no consequences, sans a "wanted" meter that increased the police force after every criminal action. DMA Designs intended the game to be played in five-minute intervals, not with an overarching story, so the traditional game goal of "beating the game" would be replaced with creating the most fulfilling, creative, and destructive experience within the environment. The city would be packed with pedestrians, abstract little bodies with big heads. Shooting, running over or otherwise killing random individuals in a successive fashion earned you bonus points. Extra rewards would be given for cops and Hare Krishna members. It took DMA Designs several years to create the complicated graphics and the unusually open world. "I sat through heated design meetings, which resulted in tears," Baglow said in a later interview. "Screaming, punches and arguments were common." The designers realized the name *Race 'n' Chase* didn't make sense now that everyone would play the bad guy. With the plethora of car stealing, they renamed it *Grand Theft Auto*.

*Grand Theft Auto* was released in November 1997. It received solid reviews and gained a small cult following on the PC. The game did not create much controversy, likely because it came out after two other violent games, the aggressive racer *Carmageddon* and bloody shootout *Postal*, and any critical mention of the title was usually evidence in the prosecution of these higher profile games. The game company Take Two acquired BMG Entertainment and supported a few spin-offs and a *GTA* sequel, but few innovations were added to the series. Jones created a few games for the new Nintendo 64 system, then sold DMA Designs to Take Two and created a new company, Real Time Worlds. He reportedly got a low six-figure amount from the DMA Designs sale to Take-Two, which would be the last known time he would get a check from the *Grand Theft Auto* series.

Prostitutes wouldn't come into the picture until Jones left the company.

■ ■ ■

Dan and Sam Houser joined BMG in the late nineties. The two London brothers grew up in their father's jazz club and would stay up late listening to vintage rap records in their bedrooms. Terry Donovan, a good friend of theirs, DJed for local techno clubs. His dad directed Robert Palmer's "Simply Irresistible" music video, which featured the middle-aged Brit in front of several pale look-alike models, wearing tight skirts and red lipstick, gyrating to his rhythm. Enamored with rock star culture, the three friends got jobs at BMG Music. They found their brief stints in concert promotion and artist representation less than glamorous. Looking for a way out, the friends jumped to BMG's newly formed interactive entertainment division. One of the first proposals to cross their desks was *Race 'n' Chase*. Dan the creative, Sam the visionary and Terry the mouthpiece all loved the idea.

BMG Entertainment was acquired by Take-Two and *Grand Theft Auto* developer DMA Designs was christened Rockstar Games. Now based in New York, Rockstar Games would throw lavish, hip-hop pumping launch parties, holding court in warehouses that could have easily had a rave party the night before. For the *Grand Theft Auto 2* party, Rockstar reportedly required guests to dial a special line, leave their phone number and, when called back, answer a random question. People were finding ecstasy pills branded with the Rockstar Games logo. Video game tastemakers openly laughed at the Rockstar crew. One major video game website wrote a scathing editorial, calling the Houser brothers and their marketing plan pretentious. People did not launch a new game with a Hollywood-style party in 1998.

David Jones left around this time. The big parties stopped. The friends stayed out of the public eye. Aside from occasional press releases, the public face of Rockstar was silent. Behind the scenes, Sam Houser would now take a much bigger production role in the next *Grand Theft Auto*. Dan Houser co-wrote the script and developed a new, intricate storyline that made heavy references to *Scarface*, Grandmaster Flash and the Furious Five, *Casino*, *The Sopranos*, Ice-T and Ice Cube. You were still playing an anonymous thug, but the world characters, from the Paul Sorvino-inspired Mafioso boss to the over-hyped gang leader, were equal to the average action movie. (The characters themselves were voiced by Robert Loggia, Joe Pantoliano and other Hollywood actors.) Nearly four years after the original game, new 3D software made it easier for Rockstar to make the experience more realistic. Gamers would experience the next *Grand Theft Auto* on the ground, not from some distant helicopter view. The game would go into widescreen when you did something particularly cool. Whether transporting a prostitute to a john or planting a bomb under a truck, each mission would feel like it was *the* climactic scene. *Grand Theft Auto III* would make any player feel like a rock star in his own movie.

Grand Theft Auto III was released for the PlayStation 2 on October 22, 2001, a few weeks after the September 11th attacks. *Grand Theft Auto III* became the subject of dozens of newspaper editorials, political discussions and PTA (Parent-Teacher Association) meetings. Some argued that, like *Doom*, it was virtual target practice for American kids. *Rolling Stone* and *Time* discussed the impact of the game. Pop culturists marveled that a video game could actually create social commentary. Game critics were equally surprised. As one *GameSpot* reviewer put it, "It's hard to believe that a game that has become an icon of the entire video game industry got its start from a primitive-looking and sounding 2D game." It quickly sold a million copies. This was well before the media caught wind of the virtual sex.

Aside from three or so female characters woven into the plotline, the only women are the prostitutes that infiltrate the city boulevards when the streetlights turn on. Often dressed in mini-skirts and halter-tops, their curves filled by jagged digital polygons, the working women will catcall from the curb if they like what you're driving. Stop your stolen car and honk the horn if you're interested. She looks around and, provided she decides to trust you, will open the passenger side and hope in. You have to find a semi-secluded area, like a dirty alleyway by the trash can, or a dim place under one of the Brooklyn Bridge-inspired infrastructures. Things won't start away once you get to a spot. You have to be patient for a second. You can't touch your joystick. Everything will go silent. Then, a barely-perceptible squeak. The car starts to rock up and down. It sounds like a trapped mouse. The controller vibrates. The hero and his entertainment remain quiet throughout. The car then abruptly stops – after one last, quick, awkward pump. "Money," one of your scores, goes down a few points, while your energy bar increases. She gets out of the car with her pay and walks away, not bothering to turn around or to further acknowledge your presence, as if trying to forget the last 15 seconds of her life. You could get your cash back by going after the prostitute and beating her to death, picking up the damp green digital money from her bloody body. Killing a series of working women might instigate a police chase, but beating one or two will rarely get their attention. By the end of 2001, as more people learned about the prostitution, the media analysis of *Grand Theft Auto III* shifted from violence to sex. The game sold even faster. No matter how gruesome the latest *Nightmare on Elm Street*, *Texas Chainsaw Massacre* or *Halloween* may have been, viewers remained just that – viewers. Nothing in modern entertainment history equaled the power to destroy a lifelike individual, in a lifelike world, with your own hands. "…[F]ar more than books or movies or music, [video] games force you to make *decisions*," Steven Johnson writes in *Everything Bad Is Good For You*. "No other pop cultural form directly engages the brain's decision-making apparatus in the same way." Unlike a film, no one else made the decision to kill off the prostitute. You did.

■ ■ ■

Well after his departure, David Jones spoke at a video game convention and admitted that the original *Grand Theft Auto* wasn't meant to be a revolutionary game. "GTA came from Pac-Man. The dots are the little people. There's me in my little, yellow car. And the ghosts are policemen." Rockstar Games had just released *Grand Theft Auto: Vice City*, a tongue-in-cheek ode to eighties Miami drug culture. The main characters wore acid-washed jean jackets and pink shirts with white suits. Actor Philip Michael Thomas, from the iconic show *Miami Vice*, played your sidekick. *Grand Theft Auto* carpeted the media. *Grand Theft Auto* parodies were done by *South Park*, *The Chappelle Show* and other cultural barometers. It was anticipated, dissected and analyzed as intensely as the latest *Harry Potter* book or a *Star Wars* movie. Politicians wanted to know what people were thinking. Parents wanted to know what their kids would be playing. Gamers wanted to know what the next level of interaction would be. *Grand Theft Auto III* had only been out for a year. Released in October 2002, *Vice City* spent the next year wrestling with *Grand Theft Auto III* for the number one spot. Critics called *Vice City* a solid, not necessarily distinctive sequel to its predecessor, a *Grand*

*Theft Auto III* update with '80s varnish. Both games were selling millions of copies at $50 each. "I think the videogame industry was actually crying out for us," Terry Donovan told *Wired*. "We don't make games about Puff-the-Fucking-Magic Dragon."

Take-Two released two other major games, the riot simulator *State of Emergency* and the driving title *Smuggler's Run*. *State of Emergency* was released in the wake of several World Trade Organization riots, the most notable one being in Seattle, but sales dropped after the initial controversy. *Smuggler's Run* was a sleeper. The Securities and Exchange Commission started investigating Take-Two for several grievances, including backdating stock options and overestimating profits. By the end of 2002, Rockstar stopped granting media interviews altogether. When it finally does a statement, it says the company is working on *Grand Theft Auto IV*, an online multiplayer game, but a later statement says the next game isn't going to be multiplayer at all, but it will be based in California.

The public silence didn't quiet the many detractors. The Playpen Gentlemen's Club in Los Angeles sued Rockstar Games for trademark violation because some of the in-game strip clubs were named "Pig Pen." They lost. Similarly, the Sex Workers Outreach Program issued a statement against the treatment of digital concubines: "Censorship is a blight on the freedoms we hold dear, but we wholeheartedly encourage citizens to vote with their dollars by refusing to purchase products which encourage the denigration and destruction of prostitutes." By then the series had already sold about 30 million copies. *Grand Theft Auto* was arguably as large as any modern pop cultural icon, so few protests or arguments against the series could realistically be to tear it down, but to raise the notoriety of the critic. Politicians and organizations realized that and, with its persistent press coverage, any affiliation to *Grand Theft Auto* would help them get their voices heard. In seven short years *Grand Theft Auto* changed from a small lightning rod to a broadcast radio signal. Each game seemed to further push the envelope and court more controversy. In a 2004 interview, it was clear that Dr. Frankenstein had no idea where his monster would attack next. "Some of it does make you grimace," David Jones said. "It is like watching GoodFellas. There are some scenes when you ask yourself, 'Did they really have to do that? How far will it go?'"

# BOYS

It is the night of the Academy Awards, and nominated writers Matt Stone and Trey Parker walk the red carpet. Stone, a thin, nerdy man in his late twenties, is wearing a peach spaghetti strap dress with additional fabric long enough to drape over his arms. It is based on 1998 Academy Award winner Gwyneth Paltrow's dress, but on him the front sags low on his droopy, underdeveloped chest. Parker, his friend and fellow co-writer and co-creator of the show *South Park*, is wearing an imitation of Jennifer Lopez's previous Academy Award outfit, a seaweed green dress that creates an open "V" from the shoulders and exposes his patchy torso down to the belly button. He usually favors a young Bill Murray, but tonight, wearing a wig with long Lopez-inspired locks and ample lip gloss, he looks like a very hirsute woman.

Nominated for Best Song (from the *South Park* movie), the two friends had just launched *South Park* three years earlier, which itself was based on a four-minute homemade short called *The Spirit of Christmas*. The film featured two school children who witness their friends get murdered by an evil, Frosty-like snowman. The Rankin-and-Bass cartoon gone wrong ends with a battle between the snowman and baby Jesus. The infant eventually decapitates the snowman by tossing his boomerang-like halo. George Clooney and other Hollywood heavy hitters supposedly passed around the video among each other and it caught the attention of Comedy Central. Stone and Parker were working at pizza chains at the time. They weren't the managers.

The twosome used the *South Park* cartoon to parody Al Qaeda leader Osama Bin Laden and President George W. Bush, African famine and the word "nigger," right-to-life icon Terry Schivo and Scientologist actor Tom Cruise, and any other controversial topic of the moment. Its closest competitor, FOX's *The Simpsons*, spent several months drawing each episode. *South Park*, with its

115

relatively crude animation and simple visuals, was written, drawn and edited within a week. Stone and Parker were able to quickly address current events. (The Terry Schivo episode, which won them an Emmy, aired the week she died.) It consistently drew more than three million viewers and became one of the most watched shows on television, surpassing Comedy Central's very popular *The Daily Show With Jon Stewart*. The audience seemed to connect to *South Park* and its fart jokes, offensive language and racy content.

America was going through a shift. The Latino population was growing almost exponentially and, because of heavy immigration and a history of having larger families, was expected to be the largest ethnic group within two decades. Affirmative action and more economic and educational opportunities put more African-Americans and women in positions of power. In 2001 Colin Powell became the first African-American Secretary of State, replacing Madeline Albright, the first female one. The same year, Clarence Thomas was appointed an Associate Justice of the Supreme Court. MTV, which once was reluctant to play Michael Jackson videos from 1982's *Thriller*, highlighted music from inner-city artists like Dr. Dre, Tupac Shakur and Sean "Diddy" Combs. The National Association for the Advancement of Colored People, or NAACP, held a press conference to discuss if its people should be called Black or African-American. Secretaries became "administrative assistants." Midgets became "little people." Ghetto-raised youths became "at-risk kids." A new term, "politically correct," or PC, became shorthand for any euphemism used to cushion judgment. While being PC was in fashion for a decade, pop cultural icons began attacking the concept as the new millennium arrived. Comedians like Chris Rock and Bill Maher and programs like *MadTV* and *South Park* took America to task for its political correctness, using biting humor and rude behavior to show that being PC just changed the language, not the actual judgments made. It relived the symptom, not the cause. If *The Simpsons*, which began in 1989, parodied how dense the typical American family was, 1996's South Park showed, despite our enlightened cultural sensitivity and new-found morals, how little we had progressed in thought – and how much we patted ourselves on the back for superficial changes in rhetoric and outward demeanor.

Video games were going through a separate, but parallel rebellion. In the early days of wood-panel Atari 2600s and lively midway arcades, Konami had a popular game with a frog crossing the road (*Frogger*), one-hit wonder Gottlieb made players hop a furry, hose-nosed monster along pyramid-shaped blocks (*Q\*bert*), and a young Nintendo established itself with a plumber dodging flaming barrels tossed by an ape (*Donkey Kong*). Fed by an open-minded audience interested in new experiences, there seemed to be no limit to what was artistically possible. Time creates standards. Joysticks began looking the same, characters fit into definable categories, and specific genres were established. There was the fast-action "twitch" shooter, the novel-like role playing game, or RPG, the action/adventure, the sports or fighting title, the first person shooter, or FPS, and the strategy game. By the time the game industry hit the billion-dollar mark, anything beyond classification rarely got on the shelf. Experimental games usually didn't get funding from publishers. It was only a matter of time before the status quo would be attacked.

In summer 2003, *60 Minutes II* visited Acclaim in its Long Island offices. The game company had made a parody of Activision's *Tony Hawk Pro Skater* series. *Tony Hawk Pro Skater* was the first sports game to give skateboarding an arcade sensibility: you could do complicated, cool-looking tricks with a few quick joystick flicks. The series had been a consistent bestseller since beginning on the Sony PlayStation in 1999. Acclaim had created its own *Tony Hawk*-inspired game, *Dave Mirra BMX*, and it failed both critically and commercially. When talks for the next *Dave Mirra BMX* began, Acclaim was experimenting with new marketing techniques. It offered new parents a significant sum of money if they named their child after its new action game, *Turok*. It reportedly started buying gravesites and real headstones to promote its undead game, *Shadowman*. Once a solid leader of arcade-to-home translations, Acclaim could now not afford another failure. With sport figure Dave Mirra's blessing, Acclaim turned its BMX game into a *Tony Hawk Pro Skater* parody. It would be called *BMX XXX*. "We wanted to do something that was different, that hasn't been done before," co-designer Ben Fischbach told *60 Minutes II* correspondent Bob Simon. "You're going to see a hooker, you're going to run into a pimp, you're going to actually carry a hooker from one point in the game to another point in the game." *60 Minutes II* had more than 10 million viewers.

*BMX XXX* begins with you doing bike stunts in a Central Park clone. During a quick run through the park you encounter a hot dog vendor who claims that someone is stealing his wieners, a can-collecting homeless man who speaks in seventies jive, a diarrhea-plagued dog, a firefighter complaining that his hose is limp and the aforementioned cursing prostitutes and their pimp, a purple-suited African-American man in stack-heel shoes and a wide leopard hat. One of the first missions is to steal the pimp's pink poodle and throw her at the diarrhea-ailed dog to distract him from pooping. Successful players are treated to a five-second animation of the digital dogs having sex, which is on par for other rewards received throughout the game. You create your own biker from scratch, from deciding a gender to the number of back tattoos. Later you can unlock more options, including topless riding, which Acclaim touts as a feature on the game's back cover (with a black bar across the offending bits). Unlike Itagaki-san's *Dead or Alive* series, there is no "jiggle factor": character breasts are round and stiff, like old bakery bread, and stand still like large, glandular rocks. You can find special tokens throughout the game, redeemable at Scores-licensed strip clubs within each level. *BMX XXX* shows a brief title screen – "Scores Manhattan: Candy" – and an even briefer dance video of the stripper on the pole. It is on par with the movie *Showgirls*, but with grainier visuals.

BMX XXX was released for the Sony PlayStation 2, Microsoft XBox and Nintendo GameCube. Wal-Mart, KB Toys and Toys 'R' Us refused to carry the title. Sony made Acclaim remove the nudity on the PlayStation 2 version. "This is a right we rarely exercise," a Sony spokesperson said. "In the case of BMX XXX, we felt that some of the game's content did not fundamentally add to the overall experience, and is therefore included purely for effect." Dave Mirra sued Acclaim three months after the game's release, claiming breach of contract, injury to reputation, unfair competition, false advertising and invasion of privacy. The extreme sports icon also asked to get his name taken off the game, saying he didn't fully realize what kind of game Acclaim was making. He sued for $21 million. Both edited and unedited versions were critical and commercial disappointments. Several critics called it the worst sports game ever made. In September 2004, Acclaim filed for Chapter 7 bankruptcy. The company was worth about $47 million, but owed $145 million. Acclaim decided to liquidate its assets and close its doors, but didn't tell its employees. "Basically, one morning we were locked out," a former employee told *Game Developer* magazine. "It was 'Don't bother coming in, they're late on their rent, once they pay it we can go back in.'" They were never let back in.

The week before Acclaim closed, a publisher called The Gathering released *The Guy Game* on the PlayStation 2 and XBox. It is a trivia game. In TitWitz, one of *The Guy Game*'s levels, you watch movie footage of one of the women at Spring Break, young, tanned and often peppy, answering a difficult question, such as, "What is the capital of Lithuania?" (Vilnius.) The game then pauses and, while you stare at the freeze frame of her chest, asks you if she gave the right answer. She often does not. Wager the correct way several times and *The Guy Game* logo, which obscures the woman's privates, begins to go transparent until she is completely nude. The corresponding "Flash-O-Meter" raises from "Soft and Squishy" to "Sorta Chubby" to its maximum length, "Super Stiff."

"I feel innovation is incredibly important in the video game industry," Jeff Spangenberg, CEO of TopHeavy, *The Guy Game* designers, said in a press release. "With *The Guy Game* we set out to do something completely different than what had been done before." *The Guy Game* did not sell many copies and did not do well with the critics, either. "So what's with a bland… party game that makes you sit through hours of girls blathering before perking up?" *Electronic Gaming Monthly* said in an editorial. "The college coeds in a certain direct-to-video series (it's wild) never had to name the current president before lifting their shirts and showing off their Dow-Corning labels."

*The Guy Game* was inspired by *Girls Gone Wild*, the direct-to-video series started by Joe Francis in 1998. While acquiring footage for various reality TV specials, the twenty-four year old noticed that freelance filmographers were mailing in an inordinate amount of live nude footage from Spring Break, Bourbon Street and other public nudity hot spots. He then realized that the girl next door strip-downs turned him on more than the average porn video. Convinced he wasn't the only person who felt that way, Francis quit his day job and began compiling what he considered the best nude clips. Going into debt, he bought late night television advertising time, hired a cameraman and hit all the major Spring Break vacation areas – Cancun, Daytona Beach, Panama – to ask women to show their chest for the camera. Often he would get them to do more. Of course, the women probably did not know about his several accusations of rape (most of them from *Girls Gone Wild* participants), the dozen lawsuits for non-consensual filming, the restraining order against him by his Santa Monica neighbor and his physical assault against a prominent journalist. Even he was surprised, he's said, at what a young woman will do for only a *Girls Gone Wild* t-shirt. (He boasts that he doesn't pay them anything.) "Francis has aimed his cameras at a generation whose notion of privacy and sexuality are different than any other," *Los Angeles Times* adult business reporter Claire Hoffman observed. "Nursed on MySpace profiles and reality television, many young people today are comfortable with being perpetually photographed and having those images on the Internet for anyone to see." The popularity of being on the series was equal to how many people were interested in watching it. The music club-style setup, where customers automatically received the next *Girls Gone Wild* movie if they *didn't* say no, was paying off. In 2002, two years before *The Guy Game*, Joe's Mantra Films Inc. sold an estimated 4.5 million tapes and DVDs. By the time *The Guy Game* was out, Joe flew his personal Gulfstream jet to scouting areas. Critics suggested he was planning on buying the Playboy empire. Francis did not dispute it.

■ ■ ■

In 2003, *Playboy* turned fifty. The magazine circulation, as high as seven million in the seventies, had plummeted down to three million readers. Additional revenue from its once popular Playboy Clubs and other brand extensions had decreased enough for the company to shut nearly all of its traditional extracurricular ventures down. Playboy told the press its focus was now going to be on new media: member-based websites, DVDs and Internet partnerships. In the early nineties, sophomoric, British "lad magazines" stormed the American shore. *Maxim, Stuff* and others were considered part of the usual publication cycle: two or three publishers will jump on the same topic, such as the home style publications *Real Simple* and *Martha Stewart Living*, or the men's tech publications *Sync* and *Cargo* in 2004, and the trend will die down in a year—leaving one or none of those magazines standing. As the new millennium came, however, the lad mags weren't disappearing. They were growing. The biggest one, *Maxim*, went to 2.5 million subscribers within a few years. Its parent company, Dennis Publishing, began racking up several prestigious magazine awards. *Playboy* and *Maxim* seemed to be on opposite trajectories.

On the cover, *Maxim* featured the latest young, thin, but curvy Hollywood actress, wearing revealing lingerie or a tight bikini. Inside were near-nude young women and features bracketed by suggested pick-up lines. No articles were over one thousand words. Recurring themes were beer, women and sports, and at least one article mentioned all three. *Maxim* appealed to a generation raised on softcore cable movies, heavily sexualized ads and free Internet porn. *Playboy*, which could have been *Maxim's* grandfather, was known for its groundbreaking journalism and hard-hitting interviews. Its risqué reputation had quite mellowed. "After *Debbie Does Dallas* or [heiress Paris Hilton's sex tape] *1 Night in Paris* – indeed, after Internet pornography – who needs Miss December 2004, flashing her little heinie at us from aboard a yacht," cultural critic Joan Acocella once said in *The New Yorker*. "One might answer that some people prefer their sexual materials softcore. If so, they can turn to the new 'lad' magazines, such as *Maxim* or *FHM*, which show the women clothed (if barely) and, at the same time, look more up-to-date than *Playboy*."

*Maxim* had the ability to sit on a college kid's coffee table, right next to *Sports Illustrated* and *Car and Driver*, while *Playboy*, with its semi-nude covers, would have to stay under the mattress next to the sticky porn collection (assuming all the porn wasn't on the laptop). *Playboy's* heavily airbrushed pictures also went against the biggest trend to affect young men's taste: *Girls Gone Wild*. Creator Joe Francis said his goal was to show the girl next door naked, something that Hugh Hefner originally said fifty years earlier, but the *Playboy* aesthetic changed in light of breast implants, Adobe Photoshop and other technological innovations. *Girls Gone Wild* fulfilled the girl next door promise, conveying youthful innocence no matter how dark things may have been behind the scenes. If *Maxim* had a home movie series, *Girls Gone Wild* would probably be it. *Playboy* was stuck between hardcore porn, which was free to anyone with an Internet connection, and the soft, virtually guilt-free visuals, which were pushed by lad magazines and R-rated movies.

One of Playboy's first new media ventures was Arush's *Playboy: The Mansion* in 2005. You play 1953 Hugh Hefner, a.k.a. Hef, with three primary goals: build the magazine empire from scratch, facilitate intellectually stimulating parties and have as much sex as possible. There are many little details, like buying office furniture, determining how much to pay models and sending out party invites. A social climber's version of *The Sims*, *Playboy: The Mansion* rewards players for making connections with the various characters in the game. You can prosper as a facilitator, with Hef introducing two people who want to work together, or as a social player, with Hef asking a woman to bed. After a brief pause, Hef will sit on the couch and watch as the woman strips down to her g-string, her round breasts and nipples as tightly wound as corduroy, and does a little stripper dance for him. (Digital Hef doesn't seem to be able to hook up with guys, as he said he did in real life.) She then straddles his lap and jumps up and down, yelping and gasping with an occasional "Wee!" It lasts for about a minute, not unlike a five-cent pony ride outside of a supermarket. The photography sequence is a bit closer to reality. True to his real-life counterpart, Hef takes all the pictures when he starts the magazine. Once a model, a photo-shoot and a backdrop is in place, you look through the viewfinder lens and snap pictures as the perky computer-controlled model makes love to the camera. The women lacked the natural curves found in 2003's *Dead or Alive Xtreme Volleyball*, and *Playboy's* biggest inspiration, *The Sims*, already had a dozen spinoffs and sold several million copies. Designer Will Wright dedicated the last decade and a half of his life to creating *Sims*-based products. It was an uphill battle on both fronts.

Arush was not the only company to do a sexy Sims-style game. For instance, in 2004 Eidos released a similar title, *Singles: Flirt Up Your Life*. *Playboy: The Mansion* had the biggest marquee value. All the games had the same results. Reviewing *Playboy: The Game*, *Electronic Gaming Monthly* wrote "Your appreciation for this game depends entirely upon your desire to see freakishly large cartoon boobs, because almost everything else in *Playboy* is a limp Sims rip-off."

■ ■ ■

In October 2004, after several years' absence, Leisure Suit Larry returned in *Leisure Suit Larry: Magna Cum Laude* for the PC, Sony PlayStation 2, Microsoft XBox and Nintendo GameCube. Al Lowe did not return with him. Sierra's new parent company, Vivendi Universal, was able to cut him out of the game development. (This was likely because of the contractual loophole created when Lowe signed the contractor agreement two decades earlier.

He had been involved in every sequel through 1996's *Leisure Suit Larry 7: Love for Sail*.) The new game featured Larry Lovage, Larry Laffer's nephew, a virgin trying to have sex on his new college campus. *Magna Cum Laude's* women had grapefruit-round mammaries and flawless skin. To hook up with someone, you have to beat several mini-games based on classic arcade titles like *Pong* or fraternity drinking staples like Quarters. (To play Quarters, you bounce a quarter off the table to make it land in a shot glass. If you miss, you take a shot. If you make it, everyone else does.) In one particular mini-game, you maneuver one of Larry's sperm through a maze of viruses. Win and the woman will strip, if not have sex with Larry. There are no overarching storylines, no strong heroines and no cheeky innuendos like the previous *Leisure Suit Larry* games. But there is a lot of nudity and cursing, two things that were heavily censored in previous games. A few months before the game's release, new *Leisure Suit Larry* producer Joshua Van Veld said that his audience was a lot more sophisticated, or at least a lot more exposed to sex, than the purchasers of the original *Larry* games. "We realize that if you can make people laugh and show lots of jiggling boobs, people will like it." *Playboy.com* reviewed the game in fall 2004, ending with "[a]lthough the game can be downright funny and sexy, veteran fans of the series won't likely appreciate the new direction, while newcomers may find that once you get past the jokes and boobs, there's not much else to keep you playing." *Electronic Gaming Monthly* gave it the "Shame of the Month" award with a 2.5 out of 10 rating average between the three reviewers. "When it comes to *Larry*," one of them noted, "abstinence sounds pretty good." Lowe himself said he admired some of the jokes in *Magna Cum Laude* ("I think the masturbating monkey addicted to cigarettes is very funny!"), but overall the game is schizophrenic: hilarious here, offensive there. He blamed the turnover of Sierra/Vivendi Universal staff mid-development for the uneven gameplay. "I have mixed emotions about *Magna Cum Laude*. It's like watching a videotape of your son recorded by his kidnapper: It's nice to see he's still alive, but under what conditions?"

The October 2004 issue of *Playboy* had its first video game centerfold, a two-page spread Luba Licious, a Larry Lovage love interest. She is wearing only a green knit cap. Luba has Kate Moss-sized arms and a 21-inch waist, both overshadowed by her wide hips, prominent bikini bottom tan and two round breasts as large as her head. A small bio lists Luba's turn-ons ("Jell-O shots, Burning Man, college professors, my roommate"), turn-offs ("the missionary position, long-term relationships, teetotalers"), and favorite book ("Kama Sutra [a.k.a. The Bible]"). *Playboy* had been taking heavy criticism for retouching and enhancing spreads for nearly two decades, since advances in desktop publishing made it easier to manipulate photos. In reference to a recent centerfold, one 2003 letter to the editor congratulated *Playboy* for making the best piece of digital art since *Shrek*. With the video game centerfolds, which would become an annual affair, *Playboy* was no longer about sexy pixies, but sexy pixels.

The following year, lad magazines *Gear* and *Loaded* closed, *FHM* went completely online and *Maxim's* circulation topped off. The *Maxim* generation was growing up and, as a result, may have become a new, younger audience for *Playboy* and its compatriots *GQ* and *Esquire*. E! Entertainment would give *Playboy* magnate Hugh Hefner and his three young girlfriends a reality TV show. Most episodes would find the Greatest Generation hero and Viagra supporter watching his two twenty-something (and one late teen) girlfriends romp around the Playboy Mansion estate, trying on different fetish clothes, throwing large parties and occasionally playing with each other. *The Girls Next Door* became E!'s number one program. Hefner spent his 80th birthday in his mansion, blowing out the candles with his three girlfriends and an audience of millions.

Joe Francis did not buy Playboy Enterprises. In 2004, the Federal Trade Commission found Mantra Films Inc. guilty of unauthorized shipping and billing. His "opt-out" subscription plan was considered deceptive. He was fined $1.1 million, half of which went back to customers. Two years later, Mantra Films Inc. lost two lawsuits, one, worth $2.1 million, for not keeping accurate age records on file and a second for filming two seventeen year old girls in Florida. In April 2007, a Reno, Nevada federal court indicted Francis on two counts of tax evasion after millions of dollars in deductions, among other major discrepancies, were found on his returns. The mogul faced up to ten years in prison.

The Gathering and TopHeavy Studios were sued four month after the release of *The Guy Game*. One of the women featured was actually a seventeen year old from South Padre Island, Texas. She wasn't an adult, which automatically made the game footage nonconsensual. In summer 2005, a judge found for the girl, deemed *The Guy Game* child pornography and ordered the title off the shelves. The Gathering recalled the remaining copies. In an attempt to recoup, the company offered a compilation DVD called *The Guy Game: Game Over!* "The rumors are true!" the game website now read. "The most controversial video game ever created – *The Guy Game* – is no longer available!" The Gathering also sold a "Special Offer": the DVD, along with a hat and t-shirt with *The Guy Game* logo. It went for forty bucks.

# ERUPTION

It all started with a Vietnamese hooker. "Me so horny. Me so hooorney. Me love you long time," she called out to the American soldiers. She says it with a strange clip, as if she was ordering miso soup instead of trying to seduce money out of GIs' pockets. It was one of several surreal moments in *Full Metal Jacket*, Stanley Kubrick's 1987 film about Vietnam. The memorable prostitute scene was bracketed by some of the most violent, disturbing war images set to film. Oliver Stone's *Platoon*, the Vietnam film from the previous year, looked like a coming-of-age movie in comparison.

As *Full Metal Jacket* hit theaters, rapper Luke Skyywalker began managing a new music group, 2 Live Crew. The California-based posse made what would later be known as bass music, bottom-heavy tunes with repetitive party lyrics and refrains. Skyywalker relocated the group to south Florida, where modern street life was cruising in sixties cars blasting trunk-rattling bass music. (The bass culture may have originated on the west coast, as reflected in California group War's 1975 hit "Low Rider," but musically shifted to Miami in the eighties.) 2 Live Crew made a couple local hits. Skyywalker felt the group still needed another hook – something to distinguish it from the thousands of other independent rap acts out there. He decided to make it the nastiest group in south Florida. In 1986, the reinvigorated act released a new album, *2 Live Crew Is What We Are*, featuring songs such as "We Want Some Pussy." It was certified gold, or 500,000 sold. A minor obscenity complaint convinced Skyywalker to release "dirty" and "clean" version of his albums: 2 Live Crew would do a non-explicit rap in the studio, then record the rap again in its original form for the explicit album. Skyywalker Records was the first hip-hop music label to offer two versions. The clean albums made it easier for radio stations to play his group's music, but it also gave Skyywalker an opportunity to be more explicit on the dirty albums. Buying the dirty version had to be a conscious choice by the consumer. In

1989 2 Live Crew released its second full-length album, *As Nasty As They Wanna Be*. The lead single was "Me So Horny."

Rap is based on found art. Synthesizers and live instrumentation have peppered rap albums since its inception, but the foundation of rap music is built on taking sixties and seventies albums, finding a short instrumental portion called a "break" or "breakbeat," and looping it so a MC can talk over it. Kids in the Bronx did not have guitars and drum kits, but they had their parents' James Brown collection and hi-fi record players. Even at the turn of this century producers talked about treasures they'd found, hard-to-find records, musty and abandoned in some random New York alleyway, that became the foundation for top ten songs. 2 Live Crew built "Me So Horny" around a brief, looped breakbeat from "Firecracker," a chunky-bass single from the late seventies dance group Mass Production.

The hedonistic calls of the disco floor were appropriated for the Reagan era. "You said it yourself, you like it like I do," Fresh Kid Ice says over the go-go beat. "Put your lips on my dick, and suck my asshole, too." The chorus is Kubrick's Vietnamese prostitute: "Ahh! Me so horny! Me love you long time!" Scratched and skipped along the breakbeat like a pebble, her recorded vocals sound like she's stuttering from a blunt trauma. "Me So Horny" became a top 40 hit. It was hard not to hear her erotic wails on major cruising strips in San Francisco, Myrtle Beach, Washington D.C. and particularly in the group's adopted hometown, Miami.

"Me So Horny" caught the ear of Florida lawyer Jack Thompson, a Christian activist and supporter of the American Family Association. He contacted Governor Bob Martinez to find out if, under state law, the album was obscene, which in turn would make selling *As Nasty As They Wanna Be* illegal in Florida. The state started a formal inquiry. In June 1990, District Court Judge Jose Gonzalez ruled that the album was legally obscene and illegal to sell. Undercover cops were dispatched to local record stores. Within a week a retailer was arrested for selling *As Nasty As They Wanna Be* to a disguised officer, not unlike a crack dealer or an unlucky john. The same week 2 Live Crew was arrested for performing the material live at a local club.

Newspapers and magazine reporters, already sensitive to amendment rights and to FOIA (Freedom Of Information Act), saw the local fight as a national battle for free speech. It was written about every week. The month following its arrest, 2 Live Crew released the equally-explicit *Banned In The U.S.A.*. The title track was a cover of "Born In The U.S.A.," Bruce Springsteen's 1984 ode to America. A Florida Appellate Court would ultimately determine that *As Nasty As They Wanna Be* was not legally obscene. On the other side of the country, the California group Niggaz Wit' Attitude, or N.W.A., had received a letter from the FBI recommending it stop promoting violence. N.W.A.'s *Straight Outta Compton* spoke of killing people as explicitly as 2 Live Crew did of sex, but the FBI specifically had issue with the song "Fuck the Police," a graphic story about police harrassment. The album was not banned, but the controversy helped sell albums. *Straight Outta Compton* and its FBI letter would give the group almost as much spotlight as the *As Nasty As They Wanna Be* obscenity ruling. In both instances, the groups realized they could be as explicit as they liked without any legal repercussions. N.W.A. would release its last album, 1991's *Efil4zaggin*, with the songs "One Less Bitch," "To Kill A Hooker," and "Appetite For Destruction." (*Efil4zaggin* was Niggaz4Life backwards.) Best-selling rapper Jay-Z once said that rap isn't just supported by minorities anymore; if you're doing better than platinum, or one million sold, white people are buying your hardcore music, too. *Banned In The U.S.A.* and *Straight Outta Compton* both went double platinum.

The success of 2 Live Crew and N.W.A. expanded the popularity of sexual rap and so-called gangsta rap. Aggressively sexual rappers Lil' Kim and Foxxy Brown would go multi-platinum in the mid nineties. N.W.A.'s Dr. Dre would dissolve the group and produce 1992's *The Chronic* and protégé Snoop Doggy Dogg's *Doggystyle*, two landmark albums that opened the door for Tupac Shakur, The Notorious B.I.G., Geto Boys, Spice 1 and numerous other gangsta rap artists. Using Skyywalker's clean and dirty system, these songs were played not only on the strip and in strip clubs, but in college dorms, at picnics and on prime time radio. Within a short period of time the number of well known hardcore sex and violence rappers tripled.

During explicit rap's rise, comedian Chris Rock released the movie *CB4*. The satire follows the adventures of aspiring rapper Albert Brown, played by Rock, and his two friends when they disown their middle- and working-class backgrounds and personify hardened criminals. In one scene, the rappers' tour bus is stopped by protesters as it arrives for a Sacramento, California concert. The group's manager stands next to the bus driver. He is wearing a blue sweatsuit, oversized glasses and a gold nameplate that reads "Trust Us." Facing the concerned group, he tells them not to worry. "To some people, these fools out here could be a problem. Bad for they image, bad for they record sales. But you brothers have created something so . . . nastay, so foul, that the iller you get, the better off we are." He flashes a Cheshire cat grin. "Now go out there, and have a good time." The scene was preceded by a montage of Billboard charts showing the group's three number one singles: "Straight Outta Locash," "Nigga Please" and "Better Than Pussy." Before paying for studio time and other costs, the average rap group may make ten percent of a ten dollar record, or one dollar per record sold. A double-platinum record like *As Nasty As They Wanna Be* or *Straight Outta Compton* could have grossed two million dollars for a group.

Rockstar Games released *Grand Theft Auto: San Andreas* in October 2004. In *San Andreas*, you play a black California ghetto teen trying to move up in rank within a local gang. Like the previous games, it rewards you for a variety of skills: careful car thievery, expert drive-by shooting, smart prostitute management. It took the remote, almost comical fantasy of *Straight Outta Compton* and making it a personal, intimate experience. "You see, we're not competing with Konami, Hasbro or Mattel," Chief Operating Officer Terry Donovan said. "We're competing with Def Jam, Adidas and New Line Cinema." Def Jam was the number one hip-hop record label. Critics called *San Andreas* the best game of 2004. *Grand Theft Auto: San Andreas* sold more than 2 million copies within the first month, grossing more than $100 million for the company.

The following summer, a fan website called GTA Garage posted a new file. It was from Patrick Wildenborg, a Dutch gamer who claimed his file would unlock something hidden in the PC version of *Grand Theft Auto: San Andreas*. "[They] decided to disable it in their final release... now you can enjoy the full experience." The game modifier was called "Hot Coffee."

In *San Andreas*, you live a virtual life in South Central Los Angeles. The main character, CJ, must exercise to stay in shape, practice firing guns to aim better, stop at burger joints to eat. He must also maintain relationships. CJ can pick up women, go on dates and even get a steady girlfriend. The storylines are cheeky – one girlfriend insists on you taking her along on a drive-by shooting – but the relationships themselves are relatively wholesome. Like its predecessors, *San Andreas'* prostitution segments are limited to the car, the squeaking shocks and vibrating joystick the only sign of intercourse. The Mature label on the box came from the violence, not the sex. After installing the Hot Coffee modifier, CJ's girlfriend will ask him in for coffee after the end of one of their dates. If you agree, the screen flashes "This is it! Gird your loins for love!" CJ follows her into the bedroom. She strips down to her thong, her naked body jagged from the rough polygons used to created it. She doesn't have any nipples. Kneeling in front of a still-clothed CJ, his girlfriend wraps her hand and mouth around the thin air in front of his designer jeans, moving her neck back and forth in the space. There isn't anything in her hand or mouth. He then puts her on the bed and gets in an awkward missionary position. He is still fully clothed. For two minutes he pumps, asking random demands like "Tell me I'm the best!" Instructions in the corner recommend pressing up and down on the joystick to get the rhythm right. A white "Excitement" bar increases or decreases based on consistent motion. Afterwards he leaves her house and the game proceeds as usual. In *San Andreas* you go to the gym and lift weights by tapping the button. If you see a bike you like, steal it and rapidly push the appropriate key to pedal faster. The game is packed with little tests of strength. As advanced as the graphics and storyline may have been, the "orgasm" bar and joystick rhythm were as simple as *Custer's Revenge* and *X-Man* on the Atari 2600. It is fucking as minigame.

Originally discovered in the PC version, Hot Coffee did not disturb many in the computer gaming community. Ten years before Hot Coffee, homemade files stripped Lara Croft of her clothes, turning *Tomb Raider* into "*Nude Raider.*" In the late seventies, when most games were not copy protected, players could get into the program code and change the game perimeters. Even as recent as 2000, the PC hit *Counter-Strike* was a user-modified version of the already popular game *Half-Life*. Developer Valve actually gave *Half-Life* players the tools to modify it.

A few weeks after Wildenborg's post, Democratic California State Assemblyman Leland Yee, a child psychologist, was told about Hot Coffee by one of his aides. Yee had tried twice – bill AB 1972 in Fall 2004 and bill AB 450 in Winter 2004 – to pass a state law that would "prohibit the sale, rent, and

THE GRAND THEFT AUTO ERA: ERUPTION

distribution of violent video games that depict serious injury to human beings in a manner that is especially heinous, atrocious, or cruel, to persons who are 16 years of age or younger… those who violate the act may be liable in an amount of up [to] $1,000 for each violation." Both were rejected. "Clearly, the video game industry is not concerned with the welfare of our children and thus it is imperative that we step in to prevent the sale of these harmful games to our children," Yee said in a press release. This was before Hot Coffee. "It's outrageous!" Yee told Rolling Stone after the file was discovered. "It tells you how to copulate a woman. That should not be in the hands of children." Yee contacted the Entertainment Software Ratings Board, the gaming equivalent of the Motion Picture Association of America, and recommended changing San Andreas's Mature rating to Adults Only. Like giving a movie an NC-17 or X rating, changing the·sticker would restrict who would carry the game. A store like Wal-Mart, already weary of the controversial game series, would no doubt stop selling it and severely cripple Rockstar's bottom line.

The game company sent a press release in July 2005, a month after Hot Coffee was publicly discovered. "We thoroughly support the work of the ESRB, and believe it has an exemplary record of rating games and promoting understanding of video game content. We also feel confident that the investigation will uphold the original rating of the game, as the work of the mod community is beyond the scope of either publisher or the ESRB." In other words, Rockstar said the pornographic segment was wholly created by a user, like a naked Lara Croft, and not by the company itself. There was no need to changed the rating. Yee blamed the ESRB. The ESRB blamed Rockstar. Rockstar blamed gamers. And someone decided to call Jack Thompson.

■ ■ ■

The objections towards Hot Coffee were built on a long history of attempts at video game legislation, though the foundation was based on violence, not sex. In 1976, Exidy released the arcade game Death Race. According to the game designer, the object was to run over gremlins with your car. A cross would appear when one of them died. The gremlins were stick figures, stick figures that could easily pass for humans. 60 Minutes ran a report on the controversial game. Many arcade owners publicly refused to carry the machine, but those that did made a killing. Regulations began the same year.

"One of the (if not the) earliest attempt at this type of regulation predated traditional computer games and occurred in Mesquite, Texas, in 1976. The city council passed an ordinance that barred anyone under the age of 17 from operating an 'amusement device' unless accompanied by a parent or guardian," Brenda Brathwaite writes in the book *Sex In Video Games*, though she notes the law was also an attempt to suffocate arcade owners who, the city believed, were affiliated with organized crime. The U.S. Supreme Court struck down the Texas law in February 1982. A decade later, Midway released *Mortal Kombat*. Unlike other popular fighting games, it featured ample blood and special "fatalities"—difficult-to-execute moves that would destroy your opponent. In one notable fatality, a strong armed fighter would lift up his enemy and rip him in half, tossing the bloody torso and wobbling legs in different directions. In 1993, Congress held hearings on video game violence. The series of school shootings, most notably Columbine in 1999, brought video games legislation back in the spotlight after it was learned the two shooters were fans of the alien shooter *Doom*. It was released in 1993 by id Software, a developer based in Mesquite, Texas.

On the early morning of June 7, 2003, Devin Moore, an eighteen year old African American, was pulled over by Fayette, Alabama, cops. Officer Arnold Strickland suspected that the car was stolen and brought him in for booking. By all accounts Moore, who had no criminal history, was cooperative until he got to the police station. According to a statement Moore made later, he grabbed Strickland's Glock and shot him twice, one time in the head. Strickland's colleague, Officer James Crump, ran down the hallway to help him and was shot three times, also one time in the head. Moore continued down the hallway, came to the door of the emergency dispatcher, and shot one Ace Mealer five times. Again, one of the five shots hit the emergency dispatcher in the head. Moore found some car keys and drove off in a police car. "Life is like a video game," he reportedly told the police after he was caught. "Everybody's got to die sometime." *60 Minutes* did a major report on the incident. Two of his victims sued Rockstar Games and related companies on the basis that Moore was a big *Grand Theft Auto* fan. The families hired Jack Thompson.

A similar case that year, in which two *Grand Theft Auto*-playing teenagers randomly killed one man and severely wounded another in Tennessee, was also taken on by Thompson. "The industry needs to cough up money so victims and their families can be compensated for their pain," he told *ABC News*. "The shareholders need to know what their games are doing to kids and their families. They need to stop pushing adult rated products to kids. These products are deadly." The lawyer was already knee-deep in *Grand Theft Auto* research when Hot Coffee became public in 2005. He began an extensive, aggressive letter writing campaign to and about the ESRB and Rockstar Games. Thompson also garnered support from powerful conservative groups such as National Institute on Media and the Family.

On July 14, 2005, Senator Hillary Rodham Clinton held a press conference to announce that she was proposing new legislation restricting video game sales. The proposed bill would prohibit the sale of violent and sexually explicit video games to minors and put in place a $5,000 penalty for those who violate the law. The ESRB technically required stores to sell Mature and Adults Only games with proof of age, but had no serious penalty for disobedient storeowners. "The disturbing material in *Grand Theft Auto* and other games like it is stealing the innocence of our children and it's making the difficult job of being a parent even harder. I am announcing these measures today because I believe that the ability of our children to access pornographic and outrageously violent material on video games rated for adults is spiraling out of control," she said.

The former First Lady actually consulted Thompson before her press conference, but she had other allies familiar with artistic law. In the early '80s, a young mother named Tipper Gore caught her twelve year old daughter playing Prince's "Darling Nikki." Horrified at lyrics like, "I knew a girl named Nikki, I guess you could say she was a sex fiend/I met her in a hotel lobby, masturbating with a magazine," Gore talked with her Tennessee congressman husband, Al, as well as the wives of the U.S. Secretary of Treasury James Baker and South Carolina Senator Strom Thurmond. In 1984 she created the Parents Music Resource Center (PMRC). Led by eight politicians' wives, the committee held rock music accountable for the increase in rape and suicides among 16 to 24 year olds in the previous three decades, citing artists such as AC/DC, Ozzy Osbourne and Blue Oyster Cult. "Since children today lack the stable family structure of past generations, they are more vulnerable to role models and authority figures outside established patriarchal institutions," she said. "I see the family as a haven of moral stability, while popular music – e.g. rock music – is a poisonous source infecting the youth of the world with messages they cannot handle." The PMRC joined forces with the National Parent-Teachers Association (PTA) and pressured the Recording Industry Association of America (RIAA) into putting a warning label on all music it deemed explicit. In 1985 the RIAA started putting a black-and-white "PARENTAL ADVISORY: EXPLICIT LYRICS" label, colloquially known as the "Tipper sticker," on objectionable albums. Wal-Mart, J.C. Penney's, and other major stores stopped carrying labeled material. Most material with a warning label was rock (rap was still relatively underground), but country and some explicit comedy albums went unlabeled. The Parental Advisory: Explicit Lyrics label did land on Frank Zappa's 1987 *instrumental* album *Jazz From Hell*. Zappa had been an outspoken critic of the PMRC a few years before. By the end of the decade presidential hopeful Bill Clinton asked Tipper's husband to become his running mate for the presidency. Al Gore served as Vice President from 1990 to 1998.

Not unlike Yee and Hot Coffee, Connecticut Democratic Senator Joseph Lieberman would learn of this new popular game, *Mortal Kombat*, through one of his aides in 1992. Disturbed by the digital violence and believing adolescents could not differentiate from fantasy and reality, Lieberman headed a series of Congressional hearings that put Nintendo and Sega to task for their home versions of *Mortal Kombat*, as well as other violent games such as the sorority-murder satire *Night Trap*. "I was startled," Lieberman would later say. "It was very violent and... rewarded violence."

Nintendo and Sega, the former the previous industry leader and the latter the gaining contender, spent most of the hearings accusing the other company of being irresponsible. Congress determined that the industry must regulate itself or a government-appointed group would regulate it. The industry created two regulatory boards, the Recreational Software Advisory Council and the Entertainment Software Rating Board, to monitor and rate every piece of retail video game software. (The ESRB would become the dominant committee within a few years.) Fearing it would alienate its customers accustomed to kid-friendly software, Nintendo removed the blood in its version of *Mortal Kombat* green. Video game editorials called the move cowardly. At the end of his vice presidency Al Gore asked Lieberman to be his running mate for his 2000 presidential bid. Talk of Lieberman in The White House launched another set of video game editorials, the argument being that his efforts over the previous decade had censored dozens of games. Some threatened not to vote for Gore because Lieberman was on the ticket. Gore lost the presidency to George W. Bush in 2000, but it is doubtful gamers had much to do with the loss. According to the U.S. Census Bureau, 18- to 24-year olds, the heart of the video game audience at the time, had the lowest voter turnout that year.

■ ■ ■

After Clinton's speech, Rockstar Games remained adamant that Hot Coffee was "the work of a determined group of hackers... They're not within our company." In the weeks since Hot Coffee was first posted, gamers worldwide used game hacking devices to explore the PlayStation 2 and XBox editions of *Grand Theft Auto: San Andreas*. Action Replay, Game Shark and other legal software allows you to put in codes and temporarily "hack" into a video game to get unlimited lives, weapon upgrades and other perks. It also could unlock hidden content not meant to be found.

A video of the Hot Coffee mini-game began circulating on the Internet, but it was of the PC version, and PC games, by their very nature, are modifiable. For instance, Microsoft will alert users when the latest Windows "patch" is available for download, which allows the company to correct software errors after you already bought the package at the local computer store and started using it. On the other hand, console systems at the time, like the PlayStation 2 and Xbox, had inflexible software, games that could not be modified by an outside source. Nothing could be added to the software that wasn't already there. Diligent PlayStation 2 and XBox gamers were now trying to dig through the static *San Andreas* code to see if they could unlock the sex scene revealed by Wildenborg's Hot Coffee patch. They discovered that the sex mini-game, in its entirety, was available in both the PlayStation 2 and XBox versions of *San Andreas*. People who didn't know heard through the postings on hundreds, if not thousands of video game websites. The truth was out. After spending weeks pointing at the gamer community, it was clear that the Hot Coffee mini-game had been programmed by Rockstar itself. "There is sex content in the disc," a Rockstar Games spokesperson admitted after the news broke. Insiders claim the company originally planned to include the sex mini-game, but later buried it to avoid an Adults Only rating. When dealing with millions of lines of computer code, it can be easier to hide something than to outright delete it.

The game company recalled all copies of *Grand Theft Auto: San Andreas* on American shelves, promising to re-release the original version with an Adults Only rating and a Hot Coffee-free version with the initial Mature rating. This would take weeks. Some major stores, such as Best Buy, said they weren't planning on carrying the game at all after the re-release. *GameSpot* and similar used game stores predicted heavy losses because they wouldn't be able to accept nor sell the millions of copies in circulation. *Grand Theft Auto: San Andreas* was still the number-one game in America. One analyst said that the cost of the *San Andreas* recall, including new shipments, loss of used and new game sales, and bad publicity, would be more than $50 million.

On August 6, 2005, *GameSpot* reported that, according to credible sources, the FBI was investigating death threats against Jack Thompson. One forwarded email read "For being a total fucking asshole, I think video games or [sic] freaking awesome, and they are my entire life, and for you to insult them, is like telling me my life is totally worthless. For this, sir, I AM GOING TO FUCKING KILL YOU!!!" A second email read "this is not spam, its [sic] my right as a citizen to send you thousands upon thousands of emails saying the same thing until you die painfully from gun shot wounds." A high school student was reportedly arrested for sending a few of the dozens of emails Thompson received. In November, he was barred from the Devin Moore murder case by Alabama Court Judge James Moore (no relation to the defendant) after allegedly sending harassing emails to the law firm defending Devin. "Mr. Thompson felt compelled to smear opposing counsel, other attorneys with no involvement in this case or individuals," the judge later wrote. "Mr. Thompson's actions before this court suggest that he is unable to conduct himself in a manner befitting practice in this state [of Alabama]." He still continued to write passionate letters to leaders in the video game industry. In one particularly heated correspondence, Thompson compared Entertainment Software Association head Doug Lowenstein, a Jewish man, to Adolf Hitler.

That fall the National Institute of Media and the Family published an open letter saying the organization would be distancing itself from him. It asked Thompson not to reference the association in the press. "Over the past few months, I and members of my board have a growing concern that your use of our name, without our permission, has had a negative influence as we try to educate the public to this important issue," NIMF President David Walsh said. "Your commentary has included extreme hyperbole and your tactics have included personally attacking individuals for whom I have a great deal of respect." Thompson responded with his own open letter. "Dr. Walsh's efforts are funded by Target and by a foundation run by Best Buy lawyer and Best Buy Director Elliot Kaplan. I am suing Target and Best Buy over [Rockstar's upcoming adventure] *Bully*… which both Target and Best Buy are pre-selling. You connect the dots." He added, "I am a Christian. As far as I know, Dr. Walsh is as well. There is a very clear passage in the New Testament in which believers are admonished that if they have a problem with someone, to go to that person in private and try and work it out. He didn't do that… A child psychologist who would give a heads up to Doug Lowenstein in such a matter without confronting me directly man-to-man is a person who has lost his way, in more ways than one. He is the latest casualty in an escalating war started by a reckless industry whose sociopathic [sic] poster child is [president of Rockstar Games' parent company] Paul Eibeler."

Meanwhile, Rockstar Games released *Grand Theft Auto: Liberty City Stories*, a prequel to *Grand Theft Auto III*, for Sony PSP handheld. The game was a critical and commercial success, topping sales chart despite the fact it was for a handheld game machine and was, in many ways, a retread of 2001's *Grand Theft Auto 3*. *The Warriors*, an adventure game inspired by the 1978 cult classic gang movie, came out at the same time and also sold well. During that holiday season, Clinton joined Lieberman and Indiana Senator Evan Bayh in creating the Family Entertainment Protection Act. Submitted for approval on December 16, 2005, the proposed game legislation bill would fine store managers for selling material rated inappropriate for minors by the ESRB. An independent committee would analyze the rating system annually for accuracy and consumers would have an easier time logging in complaints regarding the system. Furthermore, the Federal Trade Commission (FTC) would investigate misleading ratings and do random audits of stores to determine accessibility of adult material to minors. "This bill will help empower parents by making sure their kids can't walk into a store and buy a video game that has graphic, violent and pornographic content," Clinton said in a statement. The press release failed to mention Yee's dismissed California bills or the two other similar bills that had been shot down on a state level. Two weeks before her announcement a District Court judge found an Illinois game-restriction law unconstitutional. The previous month a District Court judge blocked a virtually identical Michigan law, saying it was "unlikely to survive strict scrutiny." Political pundits at the time said that Clinton was the most likely candidate for the Democrats' 2008 White House bid.

# BEEHIVES

The camera zooms in on a perky young woman. She looks to be in her late twenties, perhaps early thirties, and she starts talking to you about her first date: how the restaurant had to kick them out because they talked until it closed, how she looked in his eyes and could tell he was the one for her, about that instant spark, you know, the spark you feel when you click – connect – with someone. The distant strains of Natalie Cole's "Everlasting Love" – also used in the Diane Lane movie *Must Love Dogs* and other modern divorcee-looking-for-love films—begin to swell in the background. Her husband (see the ring flashing as he's gesturing?) is now talking to you about the same incident, but he has a different, complimentary interpretation. A grey-haired, honey-voiced old man begins talking to you. His face seems to take up the whole TV screen. Aren't you tired of dating, he asks. "Find your soul-mate." He tells you that eHarmony uses scientific data to match people together. There is a science, founder Dr. Neil Clark Warren implies, a science to chemistry, something his company eHarmony analyzes and gives to its subscribers. The Pew Institute's first online dating survey, released in 2006, found that one out of every three people knew someone who belonged to an online dating service and more than one in four knew someone who has gone out with a person they met online. "Nearly overnight, it seemed, dozens of similar sites emerged," *The Atlantic Monthly* wrote the same year as the survey. "Online dating became almost de rigueur for busy singles looking for love." The Los Angeles-based eHarmony alone had nine million members.

Up the coast, California developers Tom Anderson and Chris DeWolfe were also convinced social technology was going to be the next big thing. They worked within a computer company – eUniverse – and began MySpace, the first mainstream multimedia blog. (A disputed history has MySpace culling its concepts from eUniverse CEO Brad Greenspan, a man who has called himself "the true founder of MySpace.")

After a five-minute setup on MySpace, you can type in your interests, post messages and music, and make new friends who, in turn, would provide links to their personal web pages. It would be a test of six degrees of separation, the concept that every single person knew every other person in the world through a maximum of six connected people. Every personal site is one-page deep, but can scroll down as much as someone could fill it up with new friends and content. The average MySpace site would have a small box of bio information (22, Los Angeles, CA, Sagittarius), an uploaded picture serving as background (usually a personal pic or a favorite band photo) and stacks of friend "testimonials" reminiscent of high school yearbooks ("You are the kewlist! Stay sweet!"). *Wired News* called it a "highly customizable amalgam of blogging, music sharing and social-discovery services, a typical page is a near perfect reflection of the chaos and passion of youth: a music-filled space, rudely splattered with photos and covered in barely-legal prose rendered in font colors that blend together and fade into the background." MySpace grew to have seventy million users, roughly one-fourth the population size of the United States.

Geriatric mogul Rupert Murdoch bought the site for $580 million. Within weeks of the Rupert Murdoch News Corporation purchase, ABC, CBS and NBC, influential papers such as the *San Francisco Chronicle* and other major news outlets began covering MySpace in earnest – as a virtual smorgasbord for teen predators. Popular among kids, MySpace entries often gave detailed personal information, if not actual data on their location. It was like a diary open to the world. "This site," said the Connecticut Attorney General, "is a parent's worst nightmare."

MySpace was not the only site of its kind. Before MySpace was a popular networking website called Friendster, and, after MySpace, Facebook became the most discussed site. Launched in 2004 by student Mark Zuckerburg as a college networking website, Facebook grew into an older-skewing version of MySpace. *Newsweek* featured Zuckerburg on the cover. On the inside the feature story told what happened when Facebook had one of its rare maintenance shutdowns. "Over the course of those four hours I probably tried to get in five or more times. I'm addicted to Facebook," one person lamented. She was a 40-year-old mother of three.

As Facebook began, Linden Labs released the program *Second Life*. It was a 3D virtual world where you could create an avatar (a digital representation of yourself) and buy land with real money, mortgage a virtual home, get married, get drunk, make new friends, start a money-making business – in other words, you could begin and live a new life. That was it. *Second Life* was a video game with no video game in it. The virtual world remained quiet until *Wired* and other tech tastemakers began claiming *Second Life* could be "Web 2.0," the almost mythical multidimensional Internet that would take over the now dated World Wide Web. The *New York Times*, *Time* and others "discovered" the program in 2006. A woman, who's avatar name was Anshe Chung, became the first *Second Life* resident to become a millionaire in real life. (The value of the *Second Life* Linden dollar fluctuates like a real economy, but was roughly $300 Linden to every U.S. dollar in 2006.) She did it by buying up virtual real estate and flipping it for a higher price. Sony, Nike, and other companies created virtual stores with real products. Reuters opened up a *Second Life* branch. Several 2008 presidential hopefuls hopped on digital soapboxes to hold town meetings. By May 1st, 2007, *Second Life* had six million citizens (though critics argued that this figure was inflated since some people had multiple avatars).

*Second Life* visitors could actually modify the virtual world. Aside from a few restrictions, Linden Labs took a very hands-off approach to its universe. One of the first modifications was by visitor Kevin Alderman, known in-world as Stroker Serpentine. He created SexGen Platinum, a forty-five dollar modification that gave an avatar realistic genitalia and the ability to have detailed virtual sex with a partner. He would later sue another Second Lifer for stealing and distributing the applet, making it the first known lawsuit over a stolen digital dick.

A popular website called SL Escorts listed and ranked avatar prostitutes based on user feedback, linking the virtual world concubines to their real life handlers for a potential *Second Life* meet and greet. "I love all sorts of sex play from the innocent school girl… to the sex slave (with or without torture)," read an ad for one leather clad escort. "…you can just IM [instant messenger] me and I'll be very happy to content to your deepest desires!" It was followed by this itemized listing (in Linden Lab dollars):

**BLOWJOB**
L$350 with clothes
L$500 shows tits

**CYBER**
L$1,500 for half and hour
L$500 for each additional 15 minutes

**VOICE**
L$2,000 for 15 min SL voice
L$3,000 for 30 min SL voice

The developing virtual world brought new sexual ethics to the forefront, and books like Regina Lynn's *The Sexual Revolution 2.0*, Audacia Ray's *Naked on the Internet: Hookups, Downloads and Cashing In on Internet Sexploration* and Tim Guest's *Second Lives: A Journey Through Virtual Worlds* attempted to navigate what was fair in virtual love. "In the Bible it says something about thinking carnally about another woman is being unfaithful," Guest said at the time. "I don't think people nowadays would agree with that, and similarly, I think people who have online sex don't see it as cheating. It's morally okay, a pocket they can put those desires into where they won't threaten their real-life relationship."

■ ■ ■

It is a balmy Los Angeles day, and two bikini-clad women are picketing just off a major strip, shouting at any cars or people that pass. Their signs read "TOO <u>NAUGHTY</u> FOR E3." The models are from Naughty America, a multimedia porn conglomerate, and they are protesting their exclusion from the Electronic Entertainment Expo happening in the Los Angeles Convention Center behind them. The E3 organizers decided to ban so-called "booth babes," women provocatively dressed, often as video game characters, populating the various company booths. It was definitely a change of heart – the predominantly male conference allowed Rockstar Games to bring bra-and-panty strippers a few years before. Contrary to the timing, Naughty America was not saying their promotional women were why it was kicked out of E3, but because of its video game, titled *Naughty America: The Game*. The online title would allow players to hook up with others around the world.

"Sex in an online game? It's about time," the press kit said. "*Naughty America: The Game* is the first of its kind: A massive multiplayer online world that allows players to do what they've always wanted to: be naughty." After establishing a cartoon-like online persona and doing mundane things like apartment furnishing, you can go hang out in the virtual city's downtown, uptown or beach. A widely shown screenshot has a buff guy and a cute young woman dancing at the local discothèque. A less circulated picture has a chiseled blond with a mullet taking a svelte, busty redhead from behind on his mauve bedsheets. His arms are at her hips, kind of like he's steering a boat with his wrists. In the corner is a meter that reads "sexy" to "freak." It is in curvy seventies cursive. "We were very disappointed to learn of E3's stance toward *Naughty America: The Game*," the company said later. "It's the next step in social networking and online matchmaking. It's certainly not intended for everyone, but then again neither are a number of the titles featured at the show." The press called the "exclusion" a stunt (it was learned after the announcement that the company just turned in its booth paperwork too late), but the change to a more conservative conference was real. The E3 organizers was responding to events from the previous year.

Rockstar Games announced its next game, *Bully*, in 2005, setting up a preview for retailers and the press at E3. Dozens of protesters picketed in front of Take-Two headquarters in Manhattan. "This game should be banned," Liz Carnell from Bullying Online (a British website supporting bullied students) said before the event. The protesters carried signs that said "Prosecute Rockstar Games; they are felons" and "Put the cuffs on Rockstar, not youth." "I'm extremely worried that kids will play it and then act out what they've seen in the classroom…" Carnell said.

After the protest, Rockstar Games quietly announced that *Bully*, originally slated for fall 2005, would be pushed back to April 2006. It arrived on the PlayStation 2 in October 2006. In what could be described as *Grand Theft Auto Jr.*, *Bully* is an open-ended adventure at the gothic, repressive Bullworth Academy prep school. As Jimmy Hopkins, a short, freckled-faced teenager, you must navigate the various school cliques, such as the jocks, the nerds, and the preppies, and make allies to survive the school year. *Grand Theft Auto*'s guns and baseball bats are replaced with itching powder and bag o' marbles. Knuckle sandwiches are complimented by headlocks and Indian burns. The point is to humiliate foes, which, in high school, is a fate worst than death. You can also make friends. A small set of options pops up when Jimmy passes someone on campus. You can give the person a friendly nod ("Hey, how's it going?!"), a put down ("Who are you lookin' at?!") or, if you are behind him or her, a very realistic-looking wedgie. Each character will respond accordingly. A positive response gives you the option to do a courting gesture, like giving a stolen box of chocolates or a bunch of flowers uprooted from the girls' dorm front lawn. A few more flirts add a final option symbolized by two big lips. The courted will usually say something coy ("So, I'm doing this science project, and, um, we're trying to figure out if kissing helps you live longer, so, um…") and Jimmy, who seems to like being the aggressor, will grab and toss the person back, and give a long, dramatic kiss. Jimmy can do this with a girl or with a boy. The homosexual kisses did not get much media attention, especially compared to Rockstar's Hot Coffee the summer before. The early controversy over the violence, which *Bully* had very little, trumped any talks about intimacy, which *Bully* had in spades.

The *Bully* protest and the Hot Coffee fallout did not stop new, potentially controversial titles from appearing. "No fewer than six announced [online sex titles] were in development – *Spend the Night, Naughty America: The Game, Rapture Online, Heavenly Bodies, Red Light Center* and *3 Feel*," Brenda Brathwaite's *Sex in Video Games* said at the time. "Although each game had a slightly different feature set, all focused on sexual interactions between characters in the game to some degree or another." One of the most notable titles was actually in some form of public beta-testing for several years. *Sociolotron* is a massive, X-rated virtual world created by veteran game developer Patric Lagny. There are monsters to slay and treasure to find like *Ultima Online* and other adventures, but *Sociolotron* was made specifically for you to live your fantasy as a pimp, prostitute or pirate, knight, dominatrix or spy, or any other self-created design you see fit. You can then have sex with any of the hundreds of other role players on the virtual plain. If you have a desire that isn't included in the game – and there are *many* included in the game – you can ask the creator himself to code it in. It is all run by Lagny, like a mom-and-pop sex shop. He told the tech magazine *Sync*, "My intent was to fashion something the big companies, like Sony, wouldn't ever touch." Still, according to Lagny's data, female *Sociolotron* players outnumber the men almost two to one.

■ ■ ■

In 2006, authors Jon M. Gibson and Chris Carle collaborated on a line of calendars called Nerdcore. Shot by photographer Cherie Roberts, the first calendar features porn stars with video games. Miss December leans against the arcade machine of Williams' classic *Defender*, her long blonde tresses stopping just short of her ample breasts and her long legs – actually, her whole body – only covered from the calf down. She wears gym socks with gold and purple stripes. Miss November lays on her stomach across a queen-sized bed playing an old Nintendo GameBoy handheld (originally released in 1989). She twists her nude body just right so her untanned behind is in full camera view. The first edition was successful enough for Nerdcore to release a second calendar focused on superheroes. It had a launch party in a large Los Angeles comic book shop with an open bar, porn performers and blowup posters of the calendar. The tech channel G4TV and other international outlets covered the event. Masi Oka, a lead actor on the popular NBC fantasy show *Heroes*, came to the party.

The same year Evergreen Events held the first annual Sex in Video Games conference in San Francisco. "This unique conference will focus on the design, development, and technology of sex in video games from a national as well as international perspective," read the website. "In addition, this conference will also have a strong focus on business matchmaking and networking. During the conference's two day run, it will feature numerous lectures and keynotes, a machinima art show (erotic art and movies derived from video games) as well as panel discussions with leaders in video game and adult video game development." Panels included "Sex in Games: Where are We Now?,""Creating a Massively Multiplayer Online Erotic Game" and "Integrating International AO Success into the US Market". (AO stood for Adults Only.) According to the SiVG organizers, the original meeting place, the Nob Hill Masonic Center, suddenly refused to hold the conference. The venue was planned well in advance. At the last minute, the conference was moved to the Kensington Hotel. Attendees would get lost in the large building as the hoteliers did not allow the organizers to put up a sign for the conference in the lobby. MTV, *Wired*, and *The Washington Post* were able to find the event. There would be no conference in 2007.

A few months before the conference, co-organizer and Savannah College of Art & Design game design professor Brenda Brathwaite released *Sex in Video Games*. Part history lesson and part action plan, the textbook gave game designers perspective on how adult situations could improve their games. It was the first book on the topic released and is the most comprehensive listing of sex-related games available. For new developments, Brathwaite kept an online blog at *www.igda.org/sex*. In the book, Brathwaite seemed optimistic about the future of adult gaming. "While a majority of today's games seem to sport one extreme or the other – hyper-sexualized environments, avatars or actions, or nothing at all – games in the future will likely not be designed in such a way. Just as love scenes in movies are the norm and, with few exceptions, don't make headlines, so too will games find a comfortable medium."

One of the most critically acclaimed games at the time was *God of War*, a bloody, fast-paced action title based on Roman mythology. Early in the game the malevolent hero arises out of bed, leaving behind two topless women with which he presumably spent the night. While most players may have walked out of the bedroom and started the next game level, you actually have the option to come back to the bed. The women will let out an innocent giggle as the bald-headed warrior climbs in between the sheets. The camera slowly pans to a Roman vase sitting precariously on the edge of a nearby nightstand. The game shows you a series of buttons to press. Each successful hit will let out a breathless female gasp followed by a gruff hero grunt. The mini-game ends when the vase, shaken by the bed knocking, breaks on the floor. A 2007 sequel had a similar sequence in a medieval bathhouse. Both received a Mature rating, the equivalent of a movie R. The PlayStation 2 games were released by Sony, a company that, about 35 years earlier, lost the VCR war to VHS because Beta lacked porn.

Microsoft also took risks with its Mature-rated XBox 360 title *Mass Effect*, a game that was banned in Singapore before it was even released.

(The country would later lift the ban, perhaps because of pressure from the multimedia giant.) Built like a dynamic sci-fi novel, *Mass Effect* allows you to create a space military character from scratch, visit different solar systems and explore hundreds of possible storylines and outcomes. Each decision you make sends you on a different path.

The developers released early video footage of the game to the press. "I see the sadness behind your eyes," a female alien with well-braided cornrows and sensitive eyes says to you. "It tells a story that makes me want to weep. Pain and loss. But it drives you! Makes you strong. You never hide your strength, either. It serves you well, terrifies your foes. Few will dare to stand against you. This may be who you are, but this is not who you will become. It only forms the basis for your future greatness. Remember these words when doubt descends, Commander." Your character, a tough blonde with close-cropped hair, stutters over her words. The alien touches her face. "Close your eyes and relax, Commander." The game closes in on their faces, the Commander standing in front of the alien while she makes an expression of subtle ecstasy. The scene ends with a close-up of the alien's blue arm, thrown against the bedpost in a fit of passion and then sensuously brought down, as if gone limp. *Mass Effect* was released on November 20, 2007. Aside from the Singapore ban, the game did not bring any major protests or political speeches, nor were any hidden sex games or secret naked scenes revealed later. There were no million-dollar recalls nor any lawsuits from concerned parents.

Three weeks after the launch, however, Microsoft did make an official announcement: *Mass Effect* had already sold more than a million copies.

# AFTERPEEP

Do games deserve to be taken "seriously"? After three decades of sexist and racist depictions, gimmick-based erotic content and biases towards unrealistic breast sizes, maybe video games shouldn't be considered art – at least not just yet. Virtually the same argument can be placed on *modern-day* television, movies and similar media – outlets that, in some cases, have been around more than a century. It's harsh how quickly video games are judged when the measuring stick is based on mediums invented several generations ago. I would guess that thirties cinema, or sixties television, was equally bad compared to the novel.

And yet, despite its brash naïveté, video games and their virtual worlds have rapidly changed our perception of entertainment, of interaction and of human relationships. MTV has consciously shifted its already fast-paced programming to keep up with a generation raised on video games. (In fact, in 2007 it started a highly profitable MTV Games division.) Movie and television plots are more layered now because, as Steven Johnson argues in *Everything Bad Is Good For You*, video games have upped our ability to multitask and to follow multiple storylines. The way our generation uses technology to maintain relationships – through text messaging, e-mail, cell phones, social networking sites, virtual worlds and even online sex – all reflect our established comfort with this interactive medium. Its influence is almost unparalleled, and its impact on our expression – sexual or otherwise – will be seen for years to come.

As I finished editing this book in Spring 2008, Rockstar Games released *Grand Theft Auto IV*. The insanely popular game sold 5.8 million copies within its first week. Set in New York-inspired Liberty City, the adventure scored rave reviews from outlets as varied as *Variety* and *NPR*. One critic called *Grand Theft Auto IV* "the first post-modern video game," which, in my interpretation, means "the first real video game for adults." Humorously, it carries the same amount of sex, violence and satire as the previous six games, *GTA 1, 2, 3, Vice City* and *San Andreas.*

In other words, the game hasn't changed, but the perception has. And a shift in public perception, as far as the future of sexuality in video games, may be what the medium needs more than anything else.

# PORN AND PONG

# FOR FURTHER READING

Dozens of books and hundreds of articles were most helpful in writing this unusual book, but a few that were indispensable.

John D'Emilio and Estelle B. Freedman's thorough title *Intimate Matters: A History of Sexuality in America* (The University of Chicago Press, 1997) is highly recommended for more insight into American sexual history. Rarely, if ever, have I read such a clear analysis of how we've evolved over the past five centuries. It is simply breathtaking.

Legs McNeil, Jennifer Osborne and Peter Pavia's *The Other Hollywood: The Uncensored Oral History of the Porn Film Industry* (Harper Entertainment, 2006) is entertaining reading for understand the modern porn industry.

Steven Johnson's *Everything Bad Is Good for You: How Today's Popular Culture Is Actually Making Us Smarter* (Riverhead, 2005) defends the cultural value of video games, as well as modern television, in a way rarely attempted in pop culture literature.

Brenda Brathwaite's *Sex In Video Games* (Charles River Media, 2006) timelines the hundreds of bizarre, scary and occasionally great sex-related games over the past forty years, many of which weren't able to make it into my own book. Brathwaite's book is required reading for further study.

# ACKNOWLEDGEMENTS

I would like to thank three women in my life: Bernadette Johnson, Dr. Jane Briggs-Bunting and Dr. Parul Jashbai Patel. Mom, you have been my best friend and my rock, even in those times when no one seemed to believe in me, not even myself. Thank you for joining me on this journey. Jane, you were my first writing mentor, and no one pushed me as hard, or as far, as you have in the decade and a half we've known each other (and I still want you to be proud of me, even now as a grown-ass man!). You taught me that I can be tough-as-nails journalist while still remaining human, and the only limits I have are self-imposed. Thank you for being my North Star. Parul, we met when this book was in its infancy, and you stuck by my side through publishing industry politics, personal problems and even life-threatening illness. I will continue to try to love you as much as you have loved me. Thank you for being my partner.

Dad and Pop, we've had our ups and downs, but I feel that we have been able to start anew, and today I am thankful to have two wonderful role models as sensitive, yet independent-minded African-American men. I would like to be as strong of a father to my own kids someday. And to Steve Garnett, the tough Medill professor with a heart of gold! I'm so glad we were able to become mentor/mentee, and later colleagues, and it is an honor to be your friend. I still remember your support in those early days where I felt like I was just chasing my tail.

Ray and Deirdra, a guy is lucky enough to find one friend that will always be there, so having two best friends makes me feel almost undeserving. Thank you for the great feedback throughout the long process, your patience with my rough (and I mean rough) drafts and, most importantly, being part of my family through thick and thin. I love you guys.

To Kristy, it's finally done! I remember us sharing a drink at The Anvil back in '03, back when I was in such a rush to finish my writing and research, and you looked me straight in the eye and said "You have to decide: Do you want to be the first or do you want to be the best?" It took five more years, but I'm so glad I did the latter. Thank you.

To Jeanette, no one knows more about this day-to-day six year rollercoaster than you, not only because you are my closest writer friend, but also because you were going through it at the same time with your own books. I'm grateful for our friendship, and I look forward to us having more great experiences together. And don't we still have a book to write?

# ACKNOWLEDGEMENTS

To Kurt, for being one of the craziest people I've ever met. Your obnoxious rhetoric kept me happy when things were down, and your faith during this book's darkest's times helped me send out one more query, contact one more agent and write one more chapter. You are a part of this book.

Atlantic City, New Jersey is my birthplace, but I've called about a dozen other cities home since then. Thank you to Grandma Johnson, Uncle George, Aunt Freda, Mush, Noonie, and little AJ in the city and Granddad and the rest of the Brown clan in the Jersey burbs, my sisters Toni and Tiffany on the East Coast, as well as Grandma Howard, Aunt Julie and Uncle Mike in Michigan. Thank you also to fellow video game addicts Jason, Jason and Courtland, Maine and Sean, and my college buddy Mike for introducing me to *Duke Nukem 3D*, *ROTT* and every other FPS around in 1997. When I decided to go to Northwestern I had no idea how important Chicago would become, and I'd also like to acknowledge all my wonderful friends I originally met in the city who, in some way, would shape this book: my long-time buddies Meg Chilton, Liz Ganshirt and Cecily Channer, the Medill crew of Ben Jackson, Carrie Greenberg, and Katherine Glover, and fellow pop culture aficionados Melanie Rowen and Liza Pavelich (Sandy Koufax lives!). Thanks also to Shana Krochmal for being a good editor and friend, and for introducing me to Chen's Orange Chicken in Long Beach. Safe travels to Wilma Garcia, Shannon from Seattle, Great-grandmom Brown from New Orleans, Grandmom Brown, Granddad Howard and Cleveland Gillis. I look forward to seeing you guys again someday.

There are many great people who believed in this book and put in discounted, if not straight-up pro bono work into it: my readers Ray, Deirdra, Johnny, Meg, Kurt, Shana, Steve, Katherine, Parul and Martin, *Sex In Video Games* author Brenda Brathwaite, filmographer Terry "this cover will totally work!" Osterhaut (www. digitalfantastique.com), my long-time webmaster Andrew Kamm (www.nontourist. com), style and marketing maven Rachel Weingarten (www.weincountry.com), and Nerdcore calendar creator and foreword writer Jon M. Gibson (www.totallynerdcore. com). I also recognize my great editors over the years, including Scott and Chip at *Playboy*, Maribeth at *Playboy.com*, Rich at the *New York Post*, Dave and Kyle at *SPIN*, Steve at *Computer Games*, Jake and Dan at *City Link Magazine*, Pheadra at *WomenGamers.com*, Connie at *AAGamer*.com, Josh, Julie and Ed at *PlanetOut.com*, and Matthew, Cashus, Steve and Kurt at *Wireless Gaming Review/GameSpot*, as well as moral support from the soon-to-be-famous Audacia Ray (www.wakingvixen.com), the wonderful Regina Lynn (www.reginalynn.com), tech goddess Annalee Newitz (www.techsploitation.com), gaming guru Scott Steinberg, ultimate otaku Chris Kohler, spiritualist Rosemary Taylor (www.myspace.com/rorotaylor), romance authors Joan Price (www.joanprice.com) and Tina Tessina (www.tinatessina.com), indie book hero Mary Beth Temple (www.marybethtemple.com), inspirational author Jennifer Lawler (www.dojowisdom.com), my play aunt Andrea King Collier, and literally the whole staff at the American Dietetic Association—particularly Dr. Esther Myers and Jennifer Herendeen.

A big thanks to Adam Parfrey and Feral House (*www.feralhouse.com*) for taking a risk on my crazy book, to the James Fitzgerald Agency *(www.jfitzagency.com)* for having my back, to Michele Wells for being a great collaborator, to Marilyn Allen and Manie Barron for the early support and to Coop (*www.coopstuff.com*) for the spellbinding cover based on his 2006 mural, "*Atari.*"

Finally, to the city of New Orleans. I spent one incredible year in NoLa, where I wrote the bulk of this book, and I rode out a few hours before Hurricane Katrina submerged the city. The pain, suffering and neglect still breaks my heart, but they do not wash away my amazing memories of late nights, one-of-a-kind experiences and life-long friendships. Much love to chefs Sarah and Chucky (now owners of the Glass Onion in Charleston, SC, my other favorite southern city: *www.ilovetheglassonion.com*), my drinking buddy Candice, foodies Kitty and Daizee, Pete and Jenny at the barbeque shack on Poland, my NoLa family Marna and JW, rum-loving Wayne (*www.republicofrum.com*), my woadie Steve and the always-supportive Dave (fields of garlic, forever!). Most importantly, to Justin, Tracey and Pheran, and to mama Ina who took care of us during the worst storm of the century. Thank you for your love.

# SELECTED BIBLIOGRAPHY & INTERVIEWS

## SPACESHIPS

Associated Press. Atari Files Suit To Halt Blue Games. *Associated Press Wire Service.* October 15, 1982.

Blumenthal, Ralph. Porno chic: "Hard-core" grows fashionable – and very profitable. *New York Times.* January 21, 1973.

D'Emilio, John and Freedman, Estelle B. *Intimate Matters: A History of Sexuality in America.* The University of Chicago Press, 1997.

Herman, Leonard. *Phoenix: The Fall & Rise of Home Videogames.* Rolenta Press, 1994.

Kent, Steven L. *The Ultimate History of Video Games: From Pong to Pokemon – The Story Behind the Craze That Touched Our Lives and Changed the World.* Three Rivers Press, 2001.

McNeil, Legs; Osborne, Jennifer; and Pavia, Peter. *The Other Hollywood: The Uncensored Oral History of the Porn Film Industry.* Harper Entertainment, 2006.

Moriarty, Tim. Uncensored Videogames: Are Adults Ruining It For The Rest Of Us? *Videogaming and Computergaming Illustrated.* October 1983.

Russell, Diana E. *Making Violence Sexy: Feminist View On Pornography.* Taylor & Francis Group, 1993.

Schlosser, Eric. *Reefer Madness: Sex, Drugs and Cheap Labor in the American Black Market.* Mariner Books, 2004.

## PROTECTION

Abrahams, Paul. Leisure-Suit Larry's Virus Strikes Computers. *Financial Times.* November 30, 1988.

Brathwaite, Brenda. *Sex In Video Games.* Charles River Media, 2006.

Brown, Damon. Making the Atari 800 Sexy. *Computer Games.* May 2006.

Brown, Damon. PCs In Ecstasy: The Evolution of Sex in PC Games. *Computer Games.* May 2006.

Cohen, Jon. *Shots in the Dark: The Wayward Search for an AIDS Vaccine.* Norton & Company, 2001.

DeMaria, Rusel and Wilson, Johnny L. *High Score: The Illustrated History of Electronic Games (Second Edition).* McGraw-Hill Osborne Media, 2003.

Dibbell, Julian. A Rape In Cyberspace: How an Evil Clown, a Haitian Trickster Spirit, Two Wizards, and a Cast of Dozens Turned a Database Into a Society. *Village Voice.* December 23, 1993.

King, Brad and Borland, John. *Dungeons and Dreams: The Rise of Computer Game Culture from Geek to Chic.* McGraw-Hill Osborne Media, 2003.

Lowe, Al. Interview. Conducted December 11, 2004.

Moran, J.S.; Janes, H.R.; Peterman, T.A.; Stone, K.M. Increase in condom sales followings AIDS education and publicity, United States. *American Journal of Public Health.* May 1990.

Pierce, Kenneth M. Software For The Masses. *Time.* October 5, 1983.

Press, Bill. Press: The sad legacy of Jerry Falwell. *The Milford Daily News.* May 18, 2007. Available online at www.milforddailynews.com/opinion/x1987843539

Shilts, Randy. *And the Band Played On: Politics, People & the AIDS Epidemic.* St. Martin's Press, 1987.

Walsh, Arthur. Interview. Conducted March 10, 2006.

# OTAKU

*1954 Comics Code Authority.* Available online at *www.comicartville.com/comicscode.htm*

Baard, Mark. Pokey Man Big in Japan. *Wired.com.* November 24, 2001. Available online at *www.wired. com/gaming/gamingreviews/news/2001/11/48438*

Brathwaite, Brenda. *Sex In Video Games.* Charles River Media, 2006.

Crazy Legs. D3 Publishing Goes On A Friendship Adventure. *GayGamer.net.* February 15, 2005. Available online at *kotaku.com/gaming/only-in-japan/play-with-kasumis-breasts-for-25-33171.php gaygamer.net/2006/09/d3_publishing_goes_on_a_friend.html*

Crecente, Brian. Play with Kasumi's Breasts for $25. *Kotaku.com.* February 15, 2005. Available online at *kotaku.com/gaming/only-in-japan/play-with-kasumis-breasts-for-25-33171.php*

Johnstone, Bob. *We Were Burning: Japanese Entrepreneurs and the Forging of the Electronic Age.* Basic Books, 1999.

Kohler, Chris. Better than a Joystick. *Wired.* May 2003.

Kohler, Chris. Interview. Conducted January 31, 2005.

Kohler, Chris. *Power-Up: How Japanese Video Games Gave the World an Extra Life.* BradyGames, 2004.

*The Motion Picture Production Code of 1930 (Hays Code).* Available online at *www.artsreformation. com/a001/hays-code.html*

Nathan, John. *Japan Unbound: A Volatile Nation's Quest for Pride and Purpose.* Houghton Mifflin, 2004.

Sheff, David. *Game Over: How Nintendo Zapped an American Industry, Captured Your Dollars, and Enslaved Your Children.* Random House, 1993.

# VIRGINS

Brown, Damon. Strong = Sexy. *WomenGamers.com.* June 27, 2005. Available online at *www. womengamers.com/articles/strongsexy.php*

Croal, NGai and Hughes, Jane. Lara Croft, the Bit Girl. *Newsweek.* November 10, 1997.

Davis, Johnny. Techno Nation: Let The Battle Begin. *Independent on Sunday (London).* April 18, 2004.

IGN Staff. "Nude Raider" Crackdown. *IGN.com.* March 22, 1999. Available online at *pc.ign.com/ articles/067/067427p1.html*

Jenkins, David. Interview with Toby Gard. *Gamasutra.* October 23, 1998. Available online at *www. gamasutra.com/view/feature/3292/interview_with_toby_gard.php*

Kent, Steven L. *The Ultimate History of Video Games: From Pong to Pokemon – The Story Behind the Craze That Touched Our Lives and Changed the World.* Three Rivers Press, 2001.

Legal Technology. E-BUSINESS + LAW (Release.30 – 08.04.1999). *Legal Technology.* August 4, 1999. Available online at *www.legaltechnology.com/ezine/1998/ildn30.htm*

McNeil, Legs; Osborne, Jennifer; and Pavia, Peter. *The Other Hollywood: The Uncensored Oral History of the Porn Film Industry.* Harper Entertainment, 2006.

Snider, Mike. "Tomb" creator saw no profits, but has new game. *USA Today.* June 21, 2001.

# WILDFLOWERS

Chaplin, Heather and Ruby, Aaron. *Smartbomb: The Quest for Art, Entertainment, and Big Bucks in the Videogame Revolution.* Algonquin Books, 2005.

Green, Heather. Where Did All the Surfers Go? *BusinessWeek.* August 6, 2001.

Grossman, Lev. Sim Nation. *Time.* November 17, 2002.

Hirschorn, Michael. The Case for Reality TV. *The Atlantic Monthly.* May 2007.

Johnson, Steven. *Everything Bad Is Good for You: How Today's Popular Culture Is Actually Making Us Smarter.* Riverhead, 2005.

Klosterman, Chuck. *Sex, Drugs, and Cocoa Puffs: A Low Culture Manifesto.* Scribner, 2004.

Kolbert, Elizabeth. Pimps and Dragons. *The New Yorker.* May 28, 2001.

Seabrook, John. Game Master. *The New Yorker.* November 6, 2006.

*The Real World (Season Two, Episode 4).* MTV. Originally aired July 8, 1993.

# CLOSETS

*Bound*. Dino De Laurentiis Company. Theatrical release on October 4, 1996.

Bright, Susie. *Mommy's Little Girl: On Sex, Motherhood, Porn, and Cherry Pie*. Thunder's Mouth Press, 2003.

Brown, Damon. Hot Mercenary Action. *Playboy.com*. March 26, 2001.

Dignan, Joe. On-Line Game World Blocks LGBT Chats. *San Francisco Bay Times*. February 9, 2006.

Dukowitz, Gretchen. Virtually gay: the Sims is the first online game to allow gay characters. *The Advocate*. February 4, 2003.

Gerstmann, Jeff. Dark Rift for Nintendo 64 Review. *GameSpot.com*. July 10, 1997. Available online at *www.gamespot.com/n64/action/darkrift/review.html*

Liu, Stanley. Interview. Conducted March 13, 2001.

Lynn, Regina. Makin' Woohoo. *Wired.com*. October 8, 2004. Available online at *www.wired.com/culture/lifestyle/commentary/sexdrive/2004/10/65256*

McWhertor, Michael. Final Fight's Poison: A Final Word On Gender. *Kotaku.com*. December 12, 2007. Available online at *kotaku.com/gaming/capcom/final-fights-poison-the-final-word-on-gender-333130.php*

*Saturday Night Live*. NBC. Originally aired March 11, 2000.

Study uncovers MMORPG gender-swapping epidemic. *GameSpot.com*. March 5, 2008. Available online at *www.gamespot.com/pages/news/show_blog_entry.php?topic_id=26273141*

Sylvester, Sherri. Audiences debate Ellen's coming out. *CNN.com*. May 1, 1997. Available online at *www.cnn.com/SHOWBIZ/9705/01/ellen.out.reax/index.html*

Thompson, Clive. The Game of Wife. *Slate.com*. April 7, 2004. Available online at *www.slate.com/id/2098406/*

# FRANKENSTEIN

Carless, Simon. Exclusive: Rockstar Successfully Defends GTA Strip Club Lawsuit. August 2, 2006. Available online at *www.gamasutra.com/php-bin/news_index.php?story=10330*

EDGE. The Making Of... Grand Theft Auto. *EDGE*. July 2006.

Hill, Logan. Why Rockstar Games Rule. *Wired*. July 2002.

Johnson, Steven. *Everything Bad Is Good for You: How Today's Popular Culture Is Actually Making Us Smarter*. Riverhead, 2005.

Kushner, David. The Road To Ruin. *Wired*. May 2007.

Padilla, Raymond. Emerging from the Stone Age. *GameSpy.com*. Available online at *archive.gamespy.com/articles/march03/dice/jones/*

The Sunday Times. Ecosse: Big game hunter. *Times Online*. October 31, 2004. Available online at *www.timesonline.co.uk/tol/newspapers/sunday_times/scotland/article500401.ece*

# BOYS

Acocella, Joan. The Girls Next Door. *The New Yorker*. March 20, 2006.

Associated Press. 'Girls Gone Wild' company pleads guilty in sex exploitation case. *USA Today*. September 12, 2006.

Electronic Gaming Monthly. Playboy: The Mansion review. *Electronic Gaming Monthly*. April 2005.

Electronic Gaming Monthly. Leisure Suit Larry: Magna Cum Laude review. *Electronic Gaming Monthly*. December 2004.

Elliot, Shawn. EGM's Third Annual Tobias Bruckner Memorial Awards For Excellence In The Field Of Crapulence. *Electronic Gaming Monthly*. March 2005.

Federal Trade Commission. Sellers of 'Girls Gone Wild' Videos to Pay $1.1 Million to Settle Charges of Unauthorized Shipping and Billing. *Federal Trade Commision*. July 30, 2004. Available online at *www.ftc.gov/opa/2004/07/girlsgonewild.shtm*

Game Developer Magazine. Filing Acclaim. *Game Developer Magazine*. November 2004.

Hoffman, Claire. Joe Francis: "Baby, give me a kiss". *Los Angeles Times Magazine*. August 6, 2006.

Lowe, Al. Interview. Conducted December 11, 2004.

Official PlayStation Magazine. BMX PG-13. *Official PlayStation Magazine.* January 2003.

Playboy. Leisure Suit Larry Centerfold. *Playboy.* October 2004.

Simon, Bob. Sex, Lies and Video Games. *60 Minutes II.* August 3, 2003. Available online at *www. cbsnews.com/stories/2002/12/16/60II/main533243.shtml*

Van Veld, Joshua. Interview. Conducted May 13, 2004.

# ERUPTION

2 Live Crew. "Me So Horny". From the Luke Records album *As Nasty As They Wanna Be.* February 7, 1989.

Bradley, Ed. Can A Video Game Lead To Murder? *60 Minutes.* March 6, 2005. Available online at *www. cbsnews.com/stories/2005/03/04/60minutes/main678261.shtml*

Brathwaite, Brenda. *Sex In Video Games.* Charles River Media, 2006.

Brown, Damon. Mario As Suge Knight. *AAGamer.com.* March 5, 2005.

*CB4.* Universal Pictures. Theatrical release on March 12, 1993.

DeWitt, Robert. Judge denies attorney's request to withdraw from Devin Moore case. *Tuscaloosa News.* November 19, 2005. Available online at *www.tuscaloosanews.com/article/20051119/ NEWS/511190331*

Feldman, Curt. The Price of Hot Coffee: > $50 million. *GameSpot.* July 22, 2005. Available online at *www.gamespot.com/news/6129661.html*

*Full Metal Jacket.* Warner Bros. Pictures. Theatrical release on June 26, 1987.

Gamesindustry.biz. Grand Theft Auto in the dock over US road killing. *The Register.* September 11, 2003. Available online at *www.theregister.co.uk/2003/09/11/grand_theft_auto/*

Hill, Logan. Why Rockstar Games Rule. *Wired.* July 2002.

Kushner, David. Sex, Lies & Video Games. *Rolling Stone.* August 11, 2005.

Prince. "Darling Nikki". From the Warner Bros. album *Purple Rain.* June 25, 1984.

Surette, Tim; Sinclair, Brendan; and Feldman, Curt. Rumor Control Update: Bush bros. in Madden, X05 lands in Amsterdam, Revolution pics… again. *GameSpot.* August 8, 2005. Available online at *www. gamespot.com/news/2005/08/05/news_6130286.html*

# BEEHIVES

Brathwaite, Brenda. *Sex In Video Games.* Charles River Media, 2006.

Brown, Damon. "Bully" kisses the boys. *PlanetOut.* November 2006. Available online at *www.gay.com/ style/entertaining/package.html?sernum=2784&navpath=/channels/style/digital/*

Brown, Damon. Rated "X" for XBox. *PlanetOut.* December 2007. Available online at *www.gay.com/ style/package.html?coll=news_feature&sernum=5654&navpath=/channels/style/digital/&page=1*

Doig, Will. Life Swap. *Nerve.com.* 2008. Available online at *www.nerve.com/screeningroom/books/ interview_timguest/*

Feldman, Curt. Bully to blacken Rockstar's other eye? *GameSpot.* August 1, 2005. Available online at *www.gamespot.com/news/6130128.html*

Fryer, Andrea. Panel Discussion. First Annual Sex In Video Games Conference. Conducted June 8 – 9, 2006, San Francisco.

Gottlieb, Lori. How Do I Love Thee? *The Atlantic Monthly.* March 2006.

Grossman, Lev. Why Facebook Is The Future. *Time.* August 23, 2007.

Poulsen, Kevin. Scenes From the MySpace Backlash. *Wired.com.* February 27, 2006. Available online at *www.wired.com/politics/law/news/2006/02/70254*

Rider, Shawn. Dungeons and Dragons and Lacey Panties. *Sync.* April/May 2004.

Second Life Escorts. Santania Munro Profile. *SL-Escorts.com.* September 16, 2007.

# ABOUT THE AUTHOR

**Damon Brown** (*www.damonbrown.net*) writes for *Playboy*, *New York Post*, *SPIN* and *Conde Nast Portfolio*, and is a technology columnist for *PlanetOut* and *AARP Online*. He graduated from Northwestern's prestigious Masters in Magazine Publishing program and is the author of several technology guides, including *The Pocket Idiot's Guide to the iPhone*. Damon has been interviewed on CNN, NPR, BBC World and G4TV. He lives in the Bay Area, but can safely consider Atlantic City, Lansing, MI, Chicago or New Orleans his hometown.

**Jon M. Gibson** (*www.jonmgibson.com*) is the co-founder of Nerdcore, a company that released the videogame industry's very first nude pinup calendar in 2006. He also created the annual i am 8-bit exhibit, which in both provocative and intellectual ways helped to contextualize videogames as the cultural significant art form that they are.